Cancer Dreams

Cancer Dreams

Paul Winick MD

authorHOUSE®

AuthorHouse™
1663 Liberty Drive
Bloomington, IN 47403
www.authorhouse.com
Phone: 1-800-839-8640

First published by AuthorHouse 07/09/11

ISBN: 978-1-4634-1842-7 (sc)
ISBN: 978-1-4634-1841-0 (dj)
ISBN: 978-1-4634-1840-3 (ebk)

Library of Congress Control Number: 2011910235

Printed in the United States of America

Dedication

This book is dedicated to my wife Dotty, and all women who have suffered the scourge of breast cancer. Also, to all men, women and children who have battled any cancer, and to their friends and loved ones who have watched them suffer.

Chapter One

—Calling

It had only been a few days since we were told. Dotty hadn't slept, and had trouble keeping down the few morsels she had swallowed. We sat together in our bedroom where she was weeping. Over our bed hung an oil that she had painted of us looking longingly at "Moon River," named for our song. I placed my arm around her for comfort. Her once vibrant brown eyes were clouded, and her bobbed hair, which was usually impeccably coiffed, was disheveled.

I, for my part, like the typical male, tried to drive despair into hope by busying myself with details. I excused myself to go to the kitchen where my trembling hand picked up the phone to call the hospital, so I could confirm what time the next day the operation had been scheduled. Dotty was going to have the cursed "M" word, the mastectomy. My hand trembled as I picked up the phone to dial.

"Listen carefully," sang a melodious voice. *"Our prompts have changed. If this is a physician, press one now.*

"If you are calling in regard to our physician referral service, press two now."

The curly cord twisted into knots. Dotty knew how to keep it straight, knew how to keep our world in order. Not now.

"If you are calling about laboratory or X-ray results, press three now.

"If you are calling to speak to a person and know the extension, enter it now. If not, press four for the directory.

"If this call regards a billing question, press five now."

I gripped the phone, angry at the nonsense that was keeping me from Dotty's side.

"If you are inquiring about a scheduling question, press six now.
"To repeat the menu, press seven now.
"To speak to an operator, remain on the line or press zero."

My hand shook as I pressed 6. How frightened my wife must be. I was sad that we had to cancel our dream trip to Australia and New Zealand on Crystal Cruise Line. It had always been her desire to visit the lands down under, hear an opera at the Sydney Opera House, watch kangaroos and koalas frolic, and walk on a pristine blue glacier.

I missed most of the new prompts. Where was the human voice? Why did this have to take so long? Wiping sweat from my forehead, I pressed 4 to have the menu repeated.

"To schedule an appointment with one of our physicians, press one now.
"To schedule a laboratory or X-ray appointment, press two now.
"To confirm an existing appointment, press three now.
"To repeat these prompts, press four now.
"To speak to an operator, hold the line or press zero."

I just wanted to confirm what time the operation was scheduled for, what time we needed to be at the hospital. In all the confusion, I was not 100 percent sure. I heard Dotty sobbing. I called out, "I love you. Let me find out what time we need to be there tomorrow, and I'll be right back. Then I won't let you out of my arms the rest of the day."

I jabbed my middle finger into three. The once melodious voice sounded grating to me.

"To find out when your laboratory or X-ray appointment is scheduled, press one now.
"To find out when your doctor's visit is scheduled, press two now.
"To find out about a scheduled operation, press three now.
"To repeat these prompts, press four now.
"To speak to an operator, either hold the line or press zero."

Enough! I pressed O. A new singing voice said, *"Please hold the line all the operators are busy. Someone will be with you shortly."*

I bounced on the balls of my feet, then held the phone over the cradle to hang up. Enough was enough. But the information was too important so the phone remained pressed to my ear. They played Beethoven's "Ode To Joy," and I wondered what joy was left for us. I thought back on our life—the rainy night when we met.

I had called Dotty several months before, but as she was involved, we never dated. I decided to try again. "I'm glad you did. I'm no longer encumbered," she said.

Wow, she talks pretty. "Getting brung up in Brooklyn," I said, "I never loined such big woids."

Through the phone, I heard a chortle and could visualize a smile. "How would you like to take in a movie, this weekend?" I asked.

"I'd like that."

That Saturday, I had dinner at my father and stepmother's apartment in Manhattan. They were starting to pack in preparation for a move to Florida in a few months. I was borrowing my father's white DeSoto convertible, hoping it would impress Dotty.

We were on dessert, nibbling a cheesecake I had brought from Ebingers in Brooklyn. "Tell me about your date," my father said.

"Not much to tell. My roommate fixed me up. He says Dotty's bright and drop dead gorgeous. But we don't always have the same taste."

"Where did she go to school? What does she do?"

"She's a graduate of Cornell and is a high school English teacher, Pop. I haven't even taken her out once. Why the third degree?"

"Just making conversation. What's her last name?"

I smiled. "It's Isaacs, Pop. She's Jewish."

He looked at his Hamilton wrist watch and returned my smile. "You better hurry. You don't want to be late."

I realized that now that I was nearly finished with medical school, my father was ready for me to have a relationship—to bring home a nice Jewish girl. "I'm on my way," I said. "I'll bring the car back tomorrow before noon."

As I left the apartment house, wearing a crew neck sweater, a light drizzle dampened the sidewalk. Walking toward Lexington Avenue, I wondered if Dotty was as beautiful as my roommate had said.

Entering the car, I put the key in the ignition and turned. Nothing! No grinding, no churning, nothing. I pounded the wheel and tried again with the same result.

As I walked back to the apartment, the rain fell harder, forcing me to run. Standing in the lobby, waiting for the elevator, rain dripping from my hair, I tried to decide what I should do about my date. Without a car, I would have to take public transportation. That meant walking to 59th Street, taking the Lexington Avenue Line to 42nd Street, shuttling to Times Square, and then taking the IRT past Columbia University to the last stop at Van Cortland Park. It would take at least an hour and a half, and we would never make the movie on time.

As I entered the apartment, I had come to the conclusion that prudence dictated postponing the date for another time. I called Dotty, explained the situation, and rescheduled for two weeks later when I had my next weekend off without having to take call. She was disappointed, but said she understood my predicament. At least, I hoped she did. Was I acting like a spoiled brat and just being lazy at the thought of having to use public transportation? That wasn't the impression I wanted to leave with Dotty.

My father came out of the bedroom looking disheveled, his face flushed. I guessed he had plans for the evening that didn't include me being around. "What's happening?" he asked.

"The car won't start. It won't even turn over. I cancelled my date."

"That's too bad. I'm sorry about the car," my father said. "I'll get the AAA to come out in the morning."

I walked to the kitchen and poured a glass of milk. My father followed. "What are you going to do tonight?" he asked.

I shrugged. "I guess I'll take the train back to Brooklyn."

"Why don't you stay here and help us pack? You can sleep over."

I said to myself, exactly what I want to do on a Saturday night, help my father pack for a move to Florida—then sleep on the couch and probably help him pack some more the next day.

"You know, Pop, maybe I'll call Dotty back and take the train, just so I can meet her."

My father smiled. I called Dotty and asked if I could come up so we could get acquainted—maybe go out for a cup of coffee. I didn't know what to make of her hesitation, but she agreed, and gave me directions from the train station. "You can either take a cab, bus, or walk up the hill," she said.

* * *

The agonizingly annoying voice of the recording said, *"Please hold the line. All the operators are busy. Someone will be with you shortly."* I yearned to go back to Dotty, but since I heard nothing, I presumed she was sleeping. So I continued the wretched phone odyssey.

This time, I left the apartment appropriately attired, wearing a Columbia sweatshirt and a long raincoat. Lowering my head into the rain, I jogged to the station on Lexington and 59th. An hour and a half later, I got off at Van Cortland Park. It was 9:00 and I still hadn't reached Dotty's house. I decided it would be easier to walk up the hill than wait for a bus or find a cab.

Buttoning my raincoat, I ascended the hill, a fine mist bathing my face. Midway, the road forked in three directions. I stood there and wondered what Dotty meant by, "Just follow the road to Delafield Avenue." Before I decided, the heavens opened. I quickly chose the right fork and soon was soaked and hopelessly lost. There was no one around to ask directions, so I wandered searching for her house. Finally, I knocked on the door of a well-lit mansion and asked directions. They let me stand in the rain. I guessed they were afraid to let a seedy looking character like me inside, but they did point me in the right direction toward Dotty's house.

When 4500 Delafield Avenue came into view, I was too soaked and hurried to give much notice. All I saw was a two-story brick house set back on an expansive lawn. I mounted a few steps to the porch, shook off as much rainwater as I could, and then rang the doorbell.

Dotty answered as I was wiping my glasses with a handkerchief so that I could see. She had on a pleated skirt and a tight olive sweater showing off her well-endowed chest. Her slim waist and curvaceous figure caused my mouth to gape. All I could think of was the rhyme, Dotty the Body.

Dotty's inquisitive brown eyes scanned me from top to bottom. My curly hair, which I combed straight, was limp. My raincoat clung to me like a wet shower curtain, and as I shifted my weight from foot to foot, my shoes squished.

Dotty smiled. "Don't just stand there. Come in out of the rain before you catch an awful cold."

I remained so locked into the past that I hardly heard the grating voice of the recording. *"Please hold the line. All the operators are still busy. Someone will be with you shortly."* I cherished reveling in the memories, but with the future so uncertain, I hoped this wasn't all that remained for me. Just perhaps, the story of how we met, represented a new beginning, heralding the start of the rest of our lives together.

Sheepishly, I crossed the threshold. I didn't want to go any further because water was dripping off my raincoat, making puddles on the floor.

"Let me have your raincoat," Dotty said. "I'll hang it in the bathroom to dry." After she had done that, she looked at my sweatshirt. "Your shirt's soaking wet, too. Why don't I get you one of my dad's? It'll be a little small, but it's dry. I can run your sweatshirt through the dryer."

I nodded. What can she be thinking of me, I thought? I've hardly said a word.

"It's late," Dotty said. "Why don't we just stay home, sit in the living room, and chat, while your stuff is drying?"

"That would be great." *That's the best line you can come up with.*

"Would you like something to drink?" Dotty asked.

"No, thank you. I'm fine."

I followed Dotty into the living room watching her cute rear wiggle from side to side. Dotty sat on a green velour couch beckoning me to join her. "Can I sit over here?" I asked. "Velour gives me the heebie-jeebies." *Now she must think I'm a real jerk.*

"How do you like teaching?" I asked.

"I've been exposed to it my entire life. My whole family are teachers. They love it and I do too. I'm only a permanent sub, but when I finish my Master's Degree, I'll get a regular appointment."

"That's terrific." *That's the best you could come up with.*

"How do you like medical school?" she asked.

"What's to like? It's hard."

"But you want to be a doctor, don't you?"

I hesitated before nodding.

"Somehow, you're not convincing me," Dotty said.

I shrugged. "I can't think of anything else that really interests me." *I seem to be putting my foot deeper and deeper into my mouth.*

When I shivered, Dotty said, "Let me make you a cup of hot tea."

"I'd really appreciate that."

We sat around the kitchen table sipping deeply steeped Jasmine tea and nibbling on lady fingers. She only ate one. I guessed that's how she maintained her sexy figure. Not wanting to seem like a pig, I quit after two.

The conversation went from what do you do, to what do you like? "My favorite thing in the world is to read," Dotty said.

"Me too, but I haven't read a book for enjoyment in more than three years, since I started medical school." *What did I just say? Smart Paul, real smart.*

"I'm sure when you have more time, you'll get back to it."

I nodded. "What I really miss is the theater. My mom was in charge of booking Broadway shows for her Hadassah group's fund raisers. I'd get to see all the shows."

"Next to reading, that's my second favorite activity."

> *This lady is terrific. She's beautiful, sexy, bright and has a lot of the same interests I do. But she must think I'm a real jerk. I know I would feel that way if someone called me up, made a date, then broke it and twenty minutes later scheduled for the same night. I wouldn't be too happy to find a drowned rat at my door, and then having to listen to such stupid conversation would be a complete turnoff.*

Dotty washed the teacups and I dried. "It's getting late," I said.

Dotty nodded. "I'll get your stuff and drive you to the train station."

She's trying to get rid of me.

We got into Dotty's compact Valiant. It matched her figure. We didn't talk on the way to the subway. Before leaving, I was searching for the right words to say. I wished there was something snappy I could come up with to convince her to go out with me again. I mulled over several lines to let her know that I wanted to explore a possible relationship.

Before I said anything, Dotty smiled and batted her lashes. "I hope you're not going to cheat me out of that movie you promised to take me to."

I gripped the phone as the sing song voice cut off the music. *"Please hold the line. All our operators are still busy. Someone will be with you shortly."* Where is the damn operator? If they put me, a physician, through this torture, I could only imagine what my patients must feel. Images of our life flashed before me—the euphoria at the birth of our children, the proud feeling at their Bar and Bat Mitzvahs, the mixed feelings at their college graduations, our loss of their childhood superimposed on their emerging adulthood, and the anticipatory feeling I had before my recent retirement. Where have all the years gone? This was supposed to be our time.

I remembered the utter fear gripping me when she put my hand on her breast. "Does my cyst feel bigger to you?" she asked.

I moved my fingers over the lump. The once soft cyst was firmer and adhered to the skin.

"What's the matter?" she asked. "It looks like you've seen a ghost."

I shook my head. "It does feel a little different. Maybe you should go for a mammogram and sonogram."

"Paul, you're freaking me out."

"It might be nothing, but best to look into it."

"It can wait till after our Australian trip, right?"

"Let's do it now. Ease our minds. Then we can enjoy the trip. I'll call a friend and get it scheduled in the next few days."

"You're really concerned, aren't you?"

I shrugged. "Who knows?" I put my arm around her, and bent over to kiss the top of her head. "We'll see."

The tests revealed cancer, which put our lives on hold, and began a nightmare, like Odysseus trying to navigate between Scylla and Charybdis—damned if you do, damned if you don't.

I spent a few days on the phone calling colleagues and referral sources down at the university, in order to find the best surgeon for Dotty. We met and were comfortable. He seemed affable, knowledgeable and caring. He arranged for a biopsy. He removed the entire lump, which was large, cancerous, and whose outer margins showed traces of tumor. For those reasons, he recommended a mastectomy.

We spent the weekend before surgery with friends and family who visited to show support. The afternoon before surgery, we gathered with our closest relations and dearest friends at a Greek restaurant to wish Dotty luck. I hoped it didn't feel like the last supper to her.

I still waited on the phone instead of comforting Dotty. I heard her sobbing in the bedroom again. She called out for me. I squeezed the phone. "Coming," I said.

"Hello," said the operator. Dotty called to me, her voice more urgent. The operator's voice was even more lyrical than the voice on the recording. But to me it sounded like the grating sound of two unoiled gears out of synch. *"Memorial Hospital surgical scheduling. How can I help you?"*

Dotty's voice became shrill. The pathways inside my brain felt like they had been rewired. "Yes," I said. "You can help me. Take your hospital and shove it up your ass." I smashed the phone into the cradle. He may not have liked it, but I decided to call the surgeon at home that night to get the information we needed. I didn't really care at this point that other families didn't have this option. I raced down the hall toward Dotty.

Chapter Two

—Champion

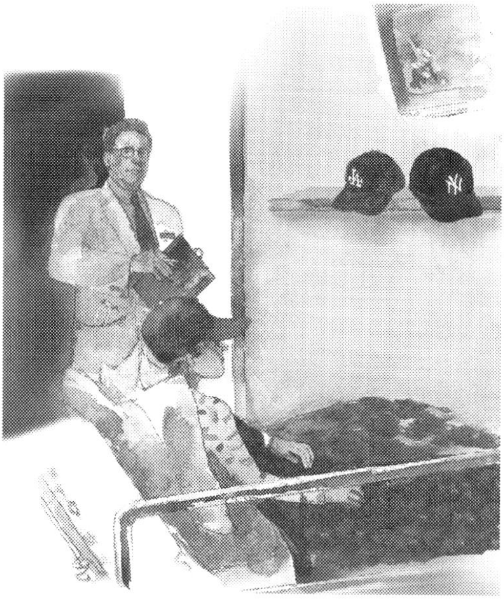

When I was young and sad, my parents would always say, everything will be better tomorrow. The sun will shine brighter. As I lay in bed, the night before Dotty's mastectomy, I hoped they were right. I prayed there would be sunshine at the end of this impending ordeal. But I feared we wouldn't emerge unscathed. Images swirled through my brain forming a movie in my mind. I stood in the center of a circle watching cancer patients I had taken care of, and friends and family members stricken with cancer, parade around me. When they stopped circling, standing before me was John, the first patient I had lost to cancer when I was a young intern. Our whole relationship crystalized before me.

John was twelve years old and like me loved baseball. When I went to visit him, he dozed in a fugue like state. The blue and white striped wallpaper merged with the blue directional stripe on the white linoleum floor, ending at his closet. His Dodger blue shirt hung next to his autographed Dodger cap.

His ghostlike face was covered with large areas of bruising. His skin was shriveled and peeling in places. John was dying—diagnosis acute myelogenous leukemia. He had undergone three unsuccessful courses of chemotherapy. There were no further treatments. My fellow interns suggested the most merciful approach would be to keep him pain free and let him die in his sleep. But they had not talked to John. He had not shared with them his dream to see his transplanted Dodgers win the pennant and the World Series.

John's father had died when he was two. I was touched that he had chosen me as his surrogate father, sharing his baseball dreams with me.

I gently woke John so that we could watch the last regular season Dodger game. Although I was a Dodger fan, I professed to being a Yankee loyalist so that I could bond with him. Now the Dodgers would be playing the Yankees in the World Series. "Hey champ," I kidded him. "Your Dodgers were lucky to win the pennant. They surely will lose to my Yankees in the world series."

When the Dodgers won the game, John shrieked with happiness. He said, "I really wanna see my Dodgers beat the pants off your Yankees. I wanna see them become champions of the world."

I vowed to do everything in my power to keep John alive so we could share the World Series together. We could at least share our love for baseball since I had no more healing skills to share with him. "See you for the series, champ. We'll watch my Yankees murder your Dodgers."

The next evening I sat at home sipping a glass of wine, listening to Beethoven's Violin Concerto, talking to Dotty, telling her about John. I was just beginning to enjoy my first leisure evening in three days, when the phone rang.

The ward nurse apologized. "Doctor, I know you're not on call, but you left orders to be notified if anything happened to John. He looks terrible.

He's pale and sweaty. His heart rate is extremely rapid. He's having trouble breathing, grunting with each respiration. He appears to be losing a lot of blood from his G.I. tract. His stools are tarry and test positive for blood."

I realized John was in heart failure caused by intestinal bleeding. The clotting factors in his blood were low.

"Please do a stat hemoglobin and hematocrit and type and cross him for three units of blood." I told the nurse. "Until the blood is available hang Ringer's Lactate in his I.V. and run it as fast as you can. I'll be right over, but if anything happens before I get there call a code. I remembered the vow I made.

The blood and I reached the ward at the same time. John looked so tired—so terminal. I knew that unless I gave him the blood rapidly, he would not survive the night. I made a surgical incision into John's ankle, and threaded a large bore catheter into the exposed Saphenous vein. I attached the blood to the catheter and hand pumped the life saving fluid into his body. By sunrise, John had received all the blood. The G.I. bleeding had stopped. He was no longer in congestive heart failure.

John opened his eyes and smiled when he saw me. "Hey, Doc, I hope we're on for the World Series tonight."

We watched all the games in his room together. We were experiencing the thrill of a potential last game together, wearing our team caps, drinking Coke, and munching pizza. I had borrowed the hat from a friend in order to keep up the charade. The Dodger's had won the first three games.

"Hey, Champ, my Dodgers will easily win this game," I kidded.

"Ain't gonna happen, Doc. The Dodgers will sweep and be world champions." I must admit that even if were a Yankee fan, I would have been rooting for the Dodgers to win.

The Dodgers clinched the championship. John fell asleep with a smile on his face, secure in the knowledge his team was a winner. His dream had been fulfilled.

Several days later, I sat at John's bedside holding one of his hands while his mother held the other. The priest had just left after administering the last rites. Rain pelted the windows and dark clouds looked like they'd release moisture forever. As my eyes filled with tears, I bid John a silent good-bye. It would be hard to lose my first patient, but I had learned more from him about courage then I had given him in return. Like his beloved Dodgers, he too was a champion. Along the way, I'd become a doctor.

I prayed Dotty's fate wouldn't be the same as John's—that there would be more time for us. I hoped the courage I had learned with John would come to the forefront now, and that I'd be able to share it with Dotty. When the alarm rang after a sleepless night, I kissed Dotty who moaned before opening her eyes. I staggered out of bed into the bathroom. It's just beginning, I thought. Please, only happy endings like my parents had taught me, but also dignity and courage like John had taught me.

Chapter Three

—Memories

At 5:30 we were in the admitting office waiting—waiting for the paperwork to be completed—waiting for transportation to arrive—waiting to be taken to the pre-op holding area. The waiting felt like it was putting a great weight on my torso. I rubbed my arms trying to relieve the spasms, but they continued unabated. Dotty, who hadn't even combed her hair, allowed her chin to sag on her chest—a soon to be lopsided chest. I didn't want her to know that I harbored such thoughts. I playfully had told her that I'm glad it's your left breast. It never was my favorite. I hoped the expander the plastic surgeon would be putting in after the mastectomy would provide an adequate cosmetic result and wouldn't leave her feeling any less about herself as a woman. This was something my older brother, Mickey, warned me about, and I was determined not to let her feel undesirable. But most of all, I prayed the operation would leave her cancer free.

A young woman came with a wheel chair to transport Dotty to the pre-op holding area. Why a wheel chair? Do they think Dotty's a cripple or will be? Do they think all cancer patients, or for that matter, anyone who needed surgery or was to be admitted, wouldn't be able to ambulate? Walking alongside, as she was being wheeled down the corridor, I wondered if this was an omen that Dotty would be physically or emotionally scarred by this ordeal. I hoped not.

When we reached our destination, there was more waiting. When we were ushered into the pre-op area itself, a nurse took a perfunctory history. Then, after Dotty was placed in a surgical gown, she mounted a gurney. She was pushed into a tiny cubicle, framed by two curtains, and hooked to wall monitors. The nurse started an I.V. through which she administered some sedation. I held Dotty's hand while she drifted in and out. The monitor had a steady drone like the beating of a metronome.—the same steady beat I hoped would be there after surgery.

Dr. Sedgeway, Dotty's surgeon, stopped in to talk, and even though Dotty nodded at what he was saying, I'm sure nothing registered. He reaffirmed what he would be doing and what the plastic surgeon would be doing after the mastectomy, when he put in an expander. Dr. Sedgeway said he'd come to speak to me in the surgical waiting room when his part of the procedure was over.

"Take good care of her," I said.

He smiled. "You bet, I will."

When they came for Dotty, I gave her the thumbs up sign, and stood watching the gurney until it was no longer visible. On the way to the waiting room, I bought some peanut butter crackers from a vending machine to munch on, and to calm my nerves, while I waited.

In the room, I stared at the T.V. without hearing or seeing anything. The movie in my mind had started up again as people circled. Stopping before me was my father, his face scrunched, as he patted his right cheek.

In 1965, Dotty and I entered the hospital to visit my father the day before he was to be operated on for the removal of a brain tumor. We held hands for comfort and for stability as Dotty was seven months pregnant. Why was this happening then—just when my father and I were forming a new adult relationship—just when he was about to have a grandchild that I hoped he would shower with the love and affection that had been lacking from him in my life? I remembered the elation I felt at the one and only baseball game he had taken me to. How excited I was that for one brief moment I could bond with him and share my love for the national past-time.

In the summer of 1947, I was nearly ten years old. We lived in Brooklyn, five blocks from Ebbett's Field and I was a rabid Dodger fan. To paraphrase a future Dodger manager, when I cut myself, I bled Dodger blue. I could quote all the statistics of the players, including their batting averages, fielding percentage, ERA's. I even knew how the prospects in the Dodger farm system were doing. My father wished I knew as much about my school work. During the season, I'd see the end of most home games because they let the kids in free after the seventh inning. I even managed to sneak into a few games after the first inning when the ticket takers weren't looking. What I had never done was to go to a game with my father. When the Dodgers were on the road, I'd be out in the street, practicing my swing with a broom handle and a Spalding ball.

That year, I had high hopes for my Dodgers bringing their first World Series back to Brooklyn. I was devastated when they lost again to the hated Yankees. My father was unsympathetic. "Why do you spend all your time on this foolishness? You'd be better off studying hard and make something of yourself—be a doctor."

"I want to be a baseball player and play for the Dodgers," I said. The look of disappointment on my father's face became ingrained in my memory. Why couldn't he understand my love for baseball?

I asked my brother why my father acted the way he did. He told me that my father had immigrated to this country at the age of eighteen, leaving his parents behind in Russia. He couldn't speak English and had no high school diploma. In seven years, going to school mostly at night and working during the day, he obtained a high school equivalency certificate, completed college and received a Master's Degree in Chemical Engineering. That's why he had no tolerance for wasting hours in non-academic pursuits. At the time, though, I didn't understand and was deeply hurt by his actions. I wished that I could share my passion for baseball with him.

When the 1948 season started, I continued badgering my father to take me to a baseball game. His response remained constant. "I don't have time for that foolishness." I pouted but didn't let that stop me from honing my skills with my trusty broom handle.

When my teacher handed me the next to last report card for the year, it didn't phase me. It was pretty much the same as all the rest. The report card was divided into two sides. On the academic side, I received outstanding for math, science and geography, and satisfactory for history, art and English. On the deportment side, I had a number of unsatisfactories, including one for conduct. In the comment section, the teacher wrote, "Runs with scissors, interrupts other children, chatters incessantly, particularly about baseball."

When I showed the report card to my father, his disapproval bore into me again. I expected him to yell. Instead, he said, "I'll tell you what I'll do, young man. On your next report card, if you get all outstandings in the academic subjects and at least satisfactory in the deportment categories, I'll take you to a baseball game."

"I will, Pop, I will."

I sneaked into fewer games and put my broom handle in the closet. I memorized dates, times, places and vocabulary words. I tried to keep my mouth shut in class, which was difficult for me. I held my breath when the teacher handed out the report cards. My hands trembled as I looked at mine. I had done it—all outstanding grades in academics and satisfactory in all aspects of deportment. The teacher wrote in the comment section, "Much improved!"

I glowed as I handed my father the report card. He did too. "You pick out the game and I'll buy the tickets, he said."

I picked a Saturday afternoon game with the Dodgers' cross town rivals, The New York Giants. I dragged my father there early on the day of game so that we could watch batting practice. He bought me popcorn and a Coke. I had already come well fortified with a box of Good-n-Plenty and a Baby Ruth bar. I hoped that I'd be able to get my father to show an interest in baseball.

We had great seats along the first base line. I had never been so close to the players. I saw Jackie Robinson, the first African American player in the major leagues, and was excited because he had been the most valuable rookie the year before. The game started and the Giants quickly jumped into the lead. My father yawned.

"Don't worry, Pop. The Dodgers will come back."

By the fifth inning, the rout was on, and my father was fast asleep. Thank goodness there was enough noise to drown out his snoring. After the seventh inning stretch, only dyed-in-the-wool fans like me remained. I guess I had mixed feelings about my father still being asleep. On the one hand, I'd get to see the whole game. He wouldn't push to leave early. On the other hand, we weren't screaming together. He wasn't sharing my love for baseball. The game was as interesting for him as watching test patterns on our new television set.

The Dodgers batted in the ninth trailing 11-2. My father continued to doze. The first batter singled up the middle, but was erased by a double play. The remaining fans edged toward the exits. Then the floodgates opened and the Dodgers' bats came to life. Soon the score was 11-6 and the Dodgers had the bases loaded. The crowd was shrieking, which woke my father.

"What's happening?" he asked.

"I told you they'd come back."

Another single, then a walk, brought the score to 11-8, and the bases were still loaded. I got up on the seat and screamed. My father stood. Another single and the score was 11-10. I howled, and to my surprise, my father said, "This is exciting."

The next batter hit a grounder to short. It's all over now, I thought, but the shortstop booted the ball, loading the bases. "We got lucky, Pop."

"We sure did." Then he screamed at the next batter. "Get a hit, you bum."

The next batter hit a screeching line drive down the third base line. It looked like the Dodgers were about to win the game when the Giants' third baseman, who was guarding the line, made a leaping catch. I felt my heart sink. The Dodgers' rally had fallen short.

I turned to my father and saw the look of disappointment on his face, the same look of disappointment I was used to when I told him I wanted to be a baseball player not a doctor. I must have had the same look too. He put his arm around me and hugged, and with his thumb wiped a tear from my eye. "I love you," he said.

I reached up and put a bear hug around his neck. "I love you too, Pop."

We walked out of the game holding hands and I waved the Dodger pennant that he had bought for me. He gently squeezed and I squeezed back.

When we walked into my father's room, he smiled. I thought, why didn't you ever take me to another game? I tried to be reassuring, but he interrupted me mid-sentence. "Of course, I'm going to be okay. Guykie's going to have a baby." He patted Dotty's stomach. "Look what I have to live for." Guykie was a term of endearment my father called Dotty. It was short for little guy, because Dotty's stature was diminutive compared to his two sons. They had bonded and became close, which had helped me improve my relationship with my father.

"You're right, Pop. Everything will be fine."

The next day, my brother and I sat with our wives in the surgical waiting room, praying for my father's recovery. I paced the floor until it felt like the leather soles on my shoes needed to be replaced. Dotty came over, put her arm around me and squeezed. I poured a cup of tea, but when I saw the neurosurgeon, I nearly spilled it. We all raced over to him.

"The surgery went fine," he said. Dad's in the recovery room. It was a benign trigeminal neuroma. We'll watch carefully, but I think he'll make an uneventful recovery,"

"Thank God," I said.

We went down to get a snack before we were allowed to see my father in the recovery room. When we arrived, he wasn't there. "They've taken him to the intensive care unit," the nurse said.

"Why, what happened?"

"Dr. Ray wants to talk to you and your brother. Let me page him."

Dr. Ray informed us that my father had a bleed in the brain post-surgery, and was on a respirator. "Things had gone so well," he said. "I don't know what happened."

Any time there's major surgery, shit can happen, I thought. "Is he going to be okay? What're his chances?"

Dr. Ray shrugged. "Who knows? Only time will tell. We'll just have to wait and see if the blood resorbs by itself, and if so how much damage your dad is left with."

At the time, I was doing a rotation on the pediatric ward of Sloane Kettering, the cancer hospital across the street from New York Hospital, where my father remained in a coma for weeks. I was grateful that no children had died the entire month I was there—that is, until my last weekend on call when I lost three children. I had to suppress my own distress to provide their families comfort—not an easy task for me in the state I was in. I hoped some resident wouldn't be doing the same thing to me when he told me of my father's death. But after three weeks of lying in a coma and not regaining consciousness that is precisely what happened. The resident said, "It was always doubtful that he'd come out of it, and if he did, he would have been seriously impaired. At least he wasn't in any pain."

He may not have been in any pain, I thought. But what about my pain? What about my pain?

The movie in my mind spun to a halt, as I opened my eyes. I stood and paced the floors, wearing down the soles of my shoes. I poured myself a cup of tea and nibbled a cookie. When Dr. Sedgeway came into the room, I nearly spilled the tea as I raced over to him.

"The surgery went fine," he said. "She's in post-op and should make an uneventful recovery. I'll look in on her later. The frozen sections showed there was no tumor left in the breast and the nodes were clean. We'll have to wait for the permanent sections of course."

I smiled. "Thank you."

I wondered how there could be no tumor left in the breast if the margins of the biopsy he had done were positive? Why did she need the mastectomy?

Dr. Sedgeway's answer, when I asked him, was to shrug. "But that's all good news." he said. "She should be fine and her prognosis is good."

I thought back to my father's surgery and a similar waiting room. Hadn't I heard all this before? This time, I hoped it would be true.

Chapter Four

—Aunt Mary

I wended my way through the maze of hallways to reach the surgical recovery room. Dotty was back on the gurney, between two curtains, hooked to monitors, and attached to dripping IV solutions. Her pallor matched the sheets. She was in a stupor, and moaned in pain. I leaned over and kissed her forehead and held her hand, but she had no realization that I was there. Nurses scurried from patient to patient, checking their vital signs and levels of consciousness. Mostly though, they sat at a desk filling out reams of paper.

Dotty looked up, licked her lips, and squinted for recognition. "Is it over?" she asked.

I nodded. But it's just beginning, I thought. "You did terrific. Dr. Sedgeway said everything went fine. He'll be in to see you when you're more alert."

Dotty put her hand on her left chest. I thought I detected a trace of sadness when she found nothing there but a bandage covering her wound and an uninflated breast expander. I was sure she wasn't thinking of the final cosmetic results, which wouldn't take place before months of inflating the expander with saline in order to make room for a permanent prosthesis.

As Dotty became more and more alert, her grimaces were replaced by guttural groans. "Let me get the nurse and see if she can give you something for the pain," I said.

The nurse injected morphine through the IV, and Dotty's eyes fluttered shut. At that moment, she looked like her Aunt Mary when she was dying of lung cancer in the same hospital. They both had the same ashen complexion.

I closed my eyes and circled my fingertips around my temples. The movie in my mind started again.

Dotty had taken her father aside. They were arguing, which was the first time I had seen that type of behavior from her when it came to her father. "Dad, how can you not go to New York? Mary's your only sister. She has no other family. She's in the hospital dying of cancer."

"I can't leave your mother and she won't travel."

"Why, on both counts?"

"She says traveling is too tiring, and with her vision, I'm afraid to leave her."

"She manages to get around fine. She's not too old or infirm."

"I know, but she can't drive."

"So what? There's a market next door, and I'll keep an eye on her while you're gone."

Dotty's father shrugged. "She gets too nervous if I'm not around."

I remembered what my father-in-law said to me when Dotty and I were married. "Now, she's yours to take care of." I guessed he felt the same way when he was married. He had a wife to take care of, so the hell with everyone else. It was a reaction I could never understand from a kind, gentle man, but he had made his wife totally dependent, and must have felt it was his cross to bear. Her sisters always wondered what had happened to that strong, independent woman.

Dotty wasn't close to her aunt, having seen her only a few times during her adult years, but she felt a strong familial obligation. When we were alone, she seemed nervous. "I have to go and see her—see if there's anything I can do. I'll stay with my mother's sisters."

"Do what you have to do. I can't get away this week, but I'll fly up next weekend."

"I'd appreciate that."

I kissed Dotty on the forehead. "If there's anything I can help you with, you know, medical or hospital stuff, call me. Otherwise, I'll help you make any final decisions when I get there."

She threw her arms around my neck, and when we separated, I wiped a tear from her eye with my thumb.

On the morning of Dotty's flight, the phone rang. I saw her nodding and jotting a note on a bedside pad. She hung up after saying she understood.

"What was that all about?" I asked.

"That was Eastern Airlines. Their plane won't make it into Fort Lauderdale. They offered me a first class ticket out of Miami at no extra cost. I agreed."

I smiled. "Smart girl. I guess you'll have to suffer through a first class flight. I'll drive you down." Typical airline foul up, I thought.

Dotty arrived in New York, and we were in constant touch. She told me that her aunt's condition had stabilized, but her cancer was terminal—it was just a matter of time. "They want to send her home, but she lives alone. Instead, they suggest a nursing home. I can't fathom that. There'll be no one here to oversee what's going on. Any ideas?"

"Let me think about it. We'll make decisions when I get there in a few days."

On the morning I was to fly to New York, the phone rang. I realized it was deja vu when an Eastern Airline representative began to speak. Their plane into Fort Lauderdale was delayed. Instead of 11:00, it wouldn't be leaving until 2:30. Typical Eastern Airlines, I thought.

I remembered when Dotty and I were flying to San Francisco to take an Alaskan cruise.

Over the Rocky Mountains, the pilot was pointing out the wonders of our country. "Look at the magnificent view outside the right windows—the snow-capped peaks on top of lush forestry. Oh, by the way, the warning light has come on showing a possible fire in one of our engines. It may just be a faulty sensor, but I'll have to shut the engine down. Don't worry though, we have enough power to land safely. As a precaution, we're going to land in Salt Lake City, so as not to risk a landing in the mountains."

I watched the flight attendants teach the crash position, and I realized this was serious business. Dotty and I held hands and squeezed as we came in for a landing. The runway was lined with emergency personnel and vehicles. There were shrieks coming from various places around the cabin. Luckily, the landing was smooth and without mishap. When we deplaned, I saw a burnt out right engine. There definitely was a fire. So it didn't surprise me that Eastern Airlines was calling to tell me about the flight delay.

When I arrived at the airport, we boarded promptly on the new schedule. I had great bulkhead seats with room to stretch my long legs. As I strapped in, the pilot's booming voice came over the intercom. "I have good news and bad news. The good news is that we have tail winds all the way to New York and should be able to make up some of the time we've lost. The bad news is that we're having a problem with our landing gear and are waiting for a part to be brought up from Miami. When it arrives, we'll leave shortly thereafter."

"No way!" I said. "Let me out of here!" I tramped off the plane pulling my carry on bag. I had no checked baggage, so I was able to catch a TWA flight without worrying about my luggage. When we landed, and my feet were on terra firma, I said to myself, thank you, God.

I looked up when Dotty stirred on the gurney and opened her eyes. "How do you feel?" I asked.

"A little better, but not good." She rubbed her chest.

A nurse came, took her vital signs and turned to me. "She's pretty stable. We'll send her up to her room soon."

I nodded. Since I was a physician who practiced at the hospital, I was able to arrange for a private room. I would be able to stay through the night. Her room consisted of a hospital bed, a few wooden chairs, and one lounge chair with a nondescript landscape hanging over it. "Where will I sleep?" I asked.

The nurse pointed to the lounger. "Over there, of course. It reclines. I'll get you a pillow and blanket."

I shrugged. Doesn't look too comfortable, I thought. But what the heck, we're not here for my comfort. I'd be fine as long as Dotty is okay.

That evening, between the nurse's aide coming in to take Dotty's vital signs, my racing to Dotty when she called out, and the lumpy lounge chair, I didn't sleep at all. In fact, in the morning, I wasn't able to straighten up because of the pain from being contorted in that chair all night.

I was stretching, when Dr. Sedgeway's nursing assistant arrived. She checked Dotty's dressing and smiled. Everything's fine. All set to go home?"

"I'm in agony," Dotty said. "I can't stand the sight of food. I even need help getting in and out of bed, just to stagger to the bathroom. How can I go home?"

"We're not doing anything here that you couldn't do at home. The insurance won't pay for another day."

"Find some way to keep her," I said.

"If that's what you want."

"Aren't you listening? That's what she wants."

"Okay then. We'll have to be creative with the diagnostic codes."

"Then be creative with the codes, just don't discharge her. By the way, have you gotten the results of the permanent sections on the lymph nodes? Was there any cancer detected in them?"

The assistant shook her head. "No, it will be a few days until we get the results back."

When she left, I stared after her. How could she even think about sending Dotty home? But I realized it wasn't her fault. That's how the system works. I remembered a patient of mine, who had undergone a similar ordeal, describe this to me as a drive by mastectomy. As a physician, I knew all too well how the system worked. I too, knew how to manipulate it, but it didn't make me happy.

My thoughts were interrupted by a nurse's aide who came to clean the toilet. When she finished, she washed her hands and then took Dotty's vital signs. I wanted to scream. You've got to be kidding. The same person who cleaned the toilet is taking vital signs. What has this hospital come to? What has my hospital come to?

Late in the morning, Dotty fell asleep after receiving some IV morphine. I sat in the uncomfortable lounge chair, and despite the discomfort, my eyelids drooped shut. The movie in my mind started again.

Stepping off the plane onto firm ground had brought immediate relief, that is, until I realized that I would be flying home on Eastern Airlines. I grabbed a cab, which sped out of Laguardia, down the Grand Central Parkway, over the Triboro bridge, and onto the East Side Drive. The Manhattan skyline spread out before me, and gave me time for reflection. I came to no conclusions about what arrangements to make for Aunt Mary. I thought my role should be to support whatever decision Dotty was comfortable with. I closed my eyes, but the blaring of horns, and the cab driver stomping on the brakes, caused me to look up. We were in front of Beth Israel Hospital, a nondescript brick edifice on the East Side, just south of Fourteenth Street. I paid the cab driver, inquired at information, and trod through the halls to meet Dotty and visit with Aunt Mary. Having arrived late, we wouldn't be meeting with her doctor until the next day.

When I reached the room, I kissed Dotty and stared at Aunt Mary. She was so pale that she almost blended into the sheets. Her face was gaunt, exaggerated by the lack of false teeth in her mouth. Her curly, gray hair with streaks of blonde was disheveled. Nasal prongs were in place delivering oxygen to her lungs. A large sign read, "No Smoking." She wouldn't be in this predicament, I thought, if she had heeded that advice years earlier.

As Aunt Mary was sleeping, I signaled Dotty to follow me into the hallway so we could talk. Outside the room, I noted for the first time, the familiar antiseptic smells of a hospital, and saw personnel sitting at the nurses station, laughing while filling out reams of paperwork. Occasionally, a nurse would look up to glance at the board to see if a patient had rung. Fat chance, I thought, that it could ever be Mary—not in her condition. She was much too weak.

"So What's happening?" I asked. "What did the doctor say?"

"It's just a question of time. Both lungs are full of cancer. He says there's nothing more to do in the hospital. She can either go home with oxygen, help, and pain killers, or go to a nursing home."

"What do you think?"

"I can't leave her here. At home, there's no one to supervise, and she has no family and few friends to visit. I don't like nursing homes. Besides, the same things hold true there. Can't we take her to Florida?"

"How are we going to do that? She's in no shape to fly on commercial airlines. Even if we buy a few first class tickets, I doubt they'll let her board in her condition—oxygen, IV's, and all that."

"Any ideas?"

I shrugged. "Some, but let's wait to talk to her doctor tomorrow. Why don't you take your mind off this for a while? Let me take you out for a nice New York dinner."

Dotty smiled. "That would be most appreciated, kind sir."

The next day, Aunt Mary's doctor confirmed everything Dotty had told me. I had called a few airlines and found out my suspicions were correct. They wouldn't let someone in Mary's condition fly commercial.

"Anything we can do to get her to Florida?" Dotty asked.

The doctor rubbed his chin. "If you could arrange for an inter-hospital transfer to one in Florida, and lease a small hospital plane to take her there, it could be accomplished."

Dotty looked at me, and I nodded. "We'll do it," I said.

I called a colleague in Florida and arranged for the transfer. Then, I found an air ambulance company willing to transport us all on a small Citation jet. It was expensive, but that didn't deter us from our decision to go ahead. An ambulance was arranged for, which would bring us to Teterboro Airport in

New Jersey where the company's jets were stationed, and an ambulance would be waiting at the other end to take us to Hollywood Memorial Hospital.

When we told Aunt Mary, she smiled and at the same time wiped a tear from her eye. She lifted up her head, which was a real effort. Her raspy voice was barely audible. "Thank you."

The next day, Aunt Mary was transferred to an ambulance and all her monitors, oxygen, and IV lines were hooked to portable equipment. On our way to Teterboro Airport, I had one arm around Dotty. The other hand held Aunt Mary's. I listened to the steady drone of the cardiac monitor and hoped it continued all the way to Florida. We stopped at Aunt Mary's apartment to pick up her elderly chihuahua. Otherwise, she refused to make the trip. When I saw the plane, I couldn't believe how small it looked. Could it really fly all the way to Florida? Were we crazy doing this?

Aunt Mary was placed in a stretcher bolted to the floor to prevent it from sliding. She clung to her dog. Dotty and I belted ourselves into the two passenger seats.

The pilot turned to us. "Everyone set?"

I nodded and stammered. "I think so."

The copilot said, "Enjoy the flight. It should be smooth till we get to Florida. A lot of storms down there. There's soft drinks and water in the cooler. Help yourself."

True to the copilot's word, the flight was smooth until we reached Florida. I had a number of soft drinks and felt like my bladder would erupt. When the plane was being buffeted from side to side in the Florida storms, I felt the rest of my body would shatter. Luckily, Aunt Mary and Dotty had dozed off. I was convinced we were out of our minds to have embarked on this course—maybe we wouldn't survive. Looking out the window, I saw lightening flashing all around, and claps of thunder drowned out the drone of the engine. The plane shook so hard that I knew what a football felt like after a shanked, wobbly punt by the kicker.

Dotty opened her eyes. "What the Hell's going on?"

"Just the usual Florida storms," I said.

The only consolation I felt was listening to the two pilots speak. "Where shall we eat, John?"

"How's about Joe's Stone Crab? I know the head waiter. No, it's closed in the summer. We'll find a place on South Beach. There's a babe I want to look up."

How could they be thinking of food and women? If my stomach hadn't been empty, I'm sure whatever was in there would have flown all over the cabin.

"Hang on tight," the pilot said. "We'll be coming in for a landing in a few minutes."

Thank God, I thought.

When the plane taxied down the runway and came to a halt, the ambulance was waiting. While Aunt Mary was being transferred, I ventured into the rain to find a bathroom, grateful that I had made it without wetting myself.

Sirens blaring, the ambulance reached the hospital in record time. After Mary was settled in her private room, it was time to leave. "We'll see you in the morning," I said. "That's when Doctor Wyman will be by to see you. They have our number at the desk. If you need anything, have them call us."

Mary ran her tongue across her lips and wheezed out a barely audible sentence. "Thank you both for everything. I couldn't bear to have been up there alone. I really appreciate you taking care of Jocko."

"No problem," I said. Funny name for a cachectic looking chihuahua, I thought.

"How's Archie? I miss my brother."

"Good," Dotty said. "I'm sure he'll be here to see you tomorrow."

That night, Dotty and I fell asleep holding hands and woke that way in the morning, neither of us having moved. We wolfed down breakfast, showered, and got ready to race to the hospital so as not to miss the doctor. Before we left, Dotty called her father to let him know we had all arrived safely. They chatted for a while before Dotty asked him what time they'd be at the hospital? She listened, said uh huh a few times, then slammed the phone into the cradle.

"What did he say?" I asked.

"He'd see us tomorrow at the hospital. He has to drive my mother to her Hadassah meeting, and wait for her."

I shook my head. "Let's go visit Mary and speak to Steve. We'd better hurry. He said he'd be there at 9:00. I know he'll take good care of Mary."

When we arrived at the hospital, Steve was seeing Aunt Mary. We took a quick look in the room and waited outside. I caught a glimpse of Mary who had more color in her face and seemed more with it. Perhaps it was due to the blood dripping into her body.

Steve came out, straightened his tie, and struck a solemn pose. "I've reviewed everything," he said. "I have to agree with her physicians in New York. She's terminal. All we can do is keep her comfortable and pain free."

"How long?" I asked. I should have known better then to ask that question. I hated it when it was asked of me.

He shrugged. "Can't answer that one. The blood seems to have made a difference. She's more lively, I'm told."

"What now?" Dotty asked.

She really doesn't have to be in the hospital. We could send her to a nursing home or to your house after arranging for oxygen and home health care."

Dotty looked at me and I nodded. We had already discussed this eventuality. "She'll come home with us, of course," Dotty said.

"I'll make arrangements," Steve said. "Let's make it for tomorrow morning. It will give you time to get her room ready, and the oxygen delivered, and I'd like to repeat her hemoglobin after she's had all the blood."

"Thank you," I said. "We really appreciate you coordinating all of this."

We went into the room to tell Aunt Mary. Animation returned to her face. "I'm so grateful," she said. "It will give us time to talk." She turned to Dotty. "Maybe I can fill you in a little about your family."

The next day we wheeled Mary to the car and brought her home. She stayed in the small guest room off the breakfast area, portable oxygen at her side. The wallpaper, green leaves on a beige background, provided a tranquil autumn setting. We spent hours around the kitchen table talking, Dotty more than me, since I had to earn a living. She was able to connect as an adult with her aunt who was forthright in telling Dotty about her hidden roots and family secrets. The dog was a great comfort to Mary and Dotty, but prevented her parents from visiting frequently as her mother was "allergic" to the dog.

After several weeks of disappointments from her brother, Mary was in a talkative mood.

"Wait till he sees my new will." She looked at Dotty. "I changed it so now you're the executrix. He'll have a fit. The money I left him will be hard for him to get, all kinds of paperwork to file and out of town banks to go to."

They then went over the terms of the will, but more important, Mary started to reveal family secrets. "Do you know how old your mother is?"

"Mid to late seventies. Two years older than my father."

Mary shook her head. "No, seven years older."

"You're kidding. That would put my mother into her eighties. Why did they hide it?"

Mary shrugged. "Maybe appearances. In those days the man was supposed to be older. We were never supposed to tell you. But there are worse things they kept hidden."

"What?"

"Did you know, my mother, your grandmother wasn't Jewish?"

"I had no idea."

"That means even though your father was brought up Jewish, went to Hebrew school, and had a Bar Mitzvah, he wasn't officially Jewish since he never converted. A Jewish child's religion is passed on through the mother's lineage not the father's. My mother and all her family are buried in Mount St. Michael's Cemetery in Queens."

Dotty had a pained look on her face. "Why would they guard that secret so closely and deprive me of some of my heritage?"

"Because your mother was ashamed to tell anyone. Nobody was to ever find out. That's why she didn't want to spend much time with me. Of course, . . ." Mary started coughing, hacked out a wad of mucous, and took a deep breath. "I'm not Jewish either, pretty much an atheist. That's why when I die I want to be cremated, and my ashes strewn over the Isaacs' family plot. No rabbis please, Just a few kind words from you or Paul."

Dotty stood, walked behind her aunt, and flung her arms around her. There were tears in both their eyes. "You know, we'll do whatever you want, but we'll have a lot more time to talk. I bet there's plenty more for me to learn about my family."

Mary started to cough again. Her lips turned blue, even as she sucked in the oxygen. "I need to lie down," Mary said.

We helped her into bed. I checked on her several times during the night and she seemed to be resting comfortably. In the morning however, we found her with shallow breathing and a thready pulse. I called 911 and the paramedics, hooked her to all the monitors, increased the amount of oxygen she was getting by using a mask, and whisked her to the hospital. After she was stabilized, I called Dotty's parents to tell them what had transpired. "We have a matinee," my father-in-law said. "We'll come to the hospital after that. Mom reminds me you promised to take us out to dinner tonight."

Isn't he listening to what I'm saying? Are a matinee and a dinner more important than your sister? "She may not be alive when you arrive." I slammed the receiver into the cradle.

Dotty and I sat in Mary's room holding her hands. She would utter an occasional guttural cry, but was no longer communicative. "I hope my father gets here before she dies," Dotty said.

I nodded.

At about 5:00, Dotty's parents arrived. Dotty filled them in as to what was happening and Mary's imminent prognosis. Mary's breathing had become shallow and rasping. We all waited lost in our own thoughts.

At about 6:00, Dotty's mother stood up. "I'm hungry. You promised to take us to dinner."

"Mom, Mary's dying. We can't leave."

Her mother scowled at her husband. "If they won't take us to dinner, Archie, then you take me downstairs to the cafeteria so that I can have a bite."

"She'll probably be dead when you come back," Dotty said.

Dotty's mother didn't say anything. She did an about face and walked toward the door. Turning back to look at Archie, she said, "Coming?"

He turned to Dotty and me, then shrugged his shoulders, started toward his wife, and walked out the door. Fifteen minutes later Mary gasped her last breath. Dotty could barely look at her parents when they returned. My thoughts ran deeper than anger. I remembered someone telling me before my marriage, if you want to know what your wife will be like in fifty years, just look at her mother. I was sure that wouldn't happen. At least, I profoundly hoped not. But one never knows.

My eyes opened wide, as Dotty yelled for me. The morphine must have worn off. She licked her lips. "Could I please have a drink of water?"

"Sure, how's about eating something, too. Lunch will be here soon."

"I'm not hungry."

"What's that got to do with it? You have to eat to get strong and all that stuff."

Her look said, you've got to be kidding.

"If you don't like the hospital fare, I'll go to the cafeteria and get you whatever you want."

She smiled. "Okay, you win. How about a grilled cheese sandwich?"

I returned her smile. "Thought that's what you'd say. That's what I ordered you for lunch, with a glass of skim milk and some caramel custard." I licked my thumb, leaned over and wiped a smudge from Dotty's forehead. "How do you feel?"

"Better, but it still hurts."

"By tomorrow that should ease considerably and you should be able to come home."

When lunch came, I helped prop Dotty in bed. As she ate, I wondered if her parents were still alive would they have visited. I guessed that it would depend on what they had to do.

Dotty spent the afternoon dozing off and on. For my part, except for a quick sojourn to get lunch, I divided my time between a hard wooden chair and the lumpy lounge chair. There was no way I was going to spend another night in that pain producing chair. My back still ached. What to do? I couldn't sleep at home and leave Dotty. I went to the nurses station to see if there was something we could do to alleviate the problem. "I'm sorry." the ward clerk said. "That's the way the rooms are set up."

I walked the ward to stretch my legs, stopping to arch my back in an effort to rid myself of the spasms. At the far end, I noted an empty room with several mattresses piled on a bed. The night nurse seemed very empathetic. Besides, I had taken care of her children. If I asked her, when she came on shift, I hoped she would let me put one of the mattresses on the floor in Dotty's room.

I was grateful that the nurse had no problem with my scheme. In fact she helped me move the mattress. That night, I slept fairly well, awakening only a few times to help Dotty.

In the morning, Dr. Sedgeway's assistant returned. "Are you ready to go home?" she asked.

Dotty nodded. "I think so."

The assistant fiddled with the dressing on Dotty's chest, then gave her some discharge instructions.

"When will I find out about the lymph nodes?" Dotty asked.

"We'll have the results when you come to the office next week."

When the assistant left, I shook my head. "Don't worry, sweetheart. I'll get the results later today or tomorrow."

The nurse came in, helped Dotty dress, then put her in a wheelchair for the trip through the hospital to the front entrance. When we arrived at the door, torrential rain was falling. Claps of thunder and bolts of lightening filled the sky. I hoped this wasn't a sign portending a poor outcome for Dotty. The weather was similar to when we had landed in the Citation jet taking Aunt Mary to Florida. I prayed Dotty's outcome would be similar to that flight, ultimately, landing on firm ground.

Chapter Five

–Peggy

The first thing Dotty did when we arrived home was to make a beeline for the bedroom. She looked so wan lying under her oil painting of Moon River. I realized it was painted in hues of reds, oranges and greens—fall colors. We were in the autumn of our years. We needed to get back to the river—to the happy times. First, we had to make sure Dotty didn't succumb to the obstacle thrown in her path.

"How do you feel?" I asked.

"Same."

"If you need anything for pain, they called in a prescription to our pharmacy. I'll pick it up later."

Dotty nodded. "Thank you."

I looked at my watch. "How about some lunch?"

Dotty scrunched her face. "Not hungry."

"Maybe some soup?"

"Okay, you win."

In the kitchen, I demonstrated the full extent of my culinary skills by opening a can of soup, emptying it into a pot, and putting the pot on the electric stove top to heat. The process would have gone faster if I had turned the burner on. Dotty smiled, as she walked into the kitchen and saw what was happening. She twisted the knob on the stove. "It'll work better this way."

I sat with Dotty at the kitchen table, blowing on the soup, searching for the right words. "Since you had the mastectomy, instead of a lumpectomy, you won't need radiation."

"I know."

"But you will need chemotherapy."

She nodded.

Dr. Sedgeway suggested we make an appointment with Dr. Wayling at the Cancer Center at Memorial. I've heard good things."

"It doesn't make me happy, but I understand."

I stood up, walked behind Dotty, and threw my arms around her. "We'll get through this fine. Just you wait and see."

Dotty excused herself to take a nap. I called up my brother and asked him to pick up Dotty's prescription when he visited later. I didn't want to leave her alone. I came into the bedroom, sat in my blue leather chair, and watched Dotty doze. I wished what I had told her, that everything would be fine, was a good prediction. Fear to the contrary gripped me—a nagging feeling that along this unchartered journey, there would be big bumps along the way. I continued watching Dotty, until my eyes closed, and I too was in the arms of Morpheus. The movie in my mind started playing.

I was in the car, driving to visit my cousin Peggy at the hospital. She was admitted with a bloated abdomen and lethargy. It made her look somewhat grotesque, as her belly was already rotund, the result of morbid obesity. Poor Peggy, I thought. Life hadn't been kind to her. I remembered back to when we were children.

Uncle Carl, Peggy's father, was a professional. Actually he was a dentist, but grandma always referred to him as a "Professional." She would always chide her younger son, Leo, to be a professional like Carl. During World War II, Carl was a fighter pilot in the Army Air Corps. After leaving the service, he opened a dental practice in Queens, in the same house in which he lived. In 1949, I was twelve years-old and Peggy was ten. That summer, we were going to see Uncle Carl in Fallsburg, New York, in the heart of the Catskill mountains. He was taking three weeks off from his busy dental practice to vacation at Grossinger's resort. We drove up Friday, after my father finished work, to visit for the weekend. The narrow two lane road cut through dense foliage. The lush maple and oak trees formed a canopy over the road, but also gave the appearance they could crush and swallow all oncoming traffic. My father had no patience for slow moving vehicles and was constantly jamming on the brakes when he was hedged in between creeping cars and approaching traffic.

"Move over, damn you!" he yelled at the car in front. "I don't have time for this foolishness." Then he stepped on the gas, whizzed past and just managed to get back in lane before colliding with an oncoming car.

By the time we reached Grossinger's, my stomach was rebelling. I got out of the car and retched. That evening at dinner, I didn't even ask for seconds.

Uncle Carl sneered at Peggy who was even fatter than me. "Ipish, I'm going to take you and Paul for a plane ride tomorrow." Ipish was not an endearing term, but in his vernacular, meant worthless. Peggy's lips quivered, but she said nothing. He looked at me. "Is that okay with you?"

Uncle Carl wanted to maintain his pilot's licence and had to fly the requisite number of hours. I was excited about going on my first plane ride, but wasn't sure my stomach was up to the occasion. I saw the flush and look of anticipation on my cousin's face and didn't want to spoil things for her. "I'd love to go, Uncle Carl, thank you." I thought Peggy was as excited about spending time with her father as she was about taking her first plane ride.

The next morning, my stomach had settled and after breakfast, we drove with my uncle to a local airport. He was driving fast and screeched onto the tarmac. I noticed he lifted his right foot from the gas and applied his left foot to the brake. How strange, I thought.

A small plane, propeller spinning, was idling on the runway. Carl laughed as Peggy tripped getting into one of the passenger seats. I struggled into the other seat, but managed to maintain balance. He gave us each a pair of goggles as we were flying in an open cockpit, and donned a brown leather flying helmet and goggles of his own. His lithe body jumped onto the wing, then into the pilot's seat. Before we were comfortable, the plane accelerated down the runway, lifted off and banked sharply to the right. I didn't have time to enjoy the scenery as my stomach rebelled again and waves of nausea took hold. I kept swallowing in an effort to keep breakfast in place. Peggy's dark complexion had taken on a greenish tinge. Uncle Carl looked around at us and smiled. His attention returned to flying and he rolled the craft until it was upside down. He descended that way and flew close to a big red barn. Breakfast was released from my stomach and pancakes, eggs, two bagels with cream cheese and various beverages flew into the air. Fortunately, the wind carried them away from the plane.

"One more pass," Uncle Carl yelled.

Peggy and I grabbed the seats, our knuckles turning white, horror on our faces. As he went over the barn upside down, I tucked my head into my chest. Pulling back up, my uncle righted the plane and brought it in for a landing.

After we had taxied off the runway over to a hanger, he jumped off the plane. "So how did you like your first ride?" he asked.

Peggy and I were too sick to answer, and Carl merely laughed. He helped us off the plane and drove back to Grossinger's like a novice race car driver trying to qualify for the Indianapolis 500. It was lucky that I had nothing left in my stomach. I spent the rest of the weekend in bed.

That fall, back in the city, I got a pulsating pain in a molar that had just erupted. I was alone in the house. Taking aspirin and sucking ice didn't dampen the pain. The throbbing intensified. I called my mother at her Hadassah meeting, but she had already left to have lunch with my aunt. I called Uncle Carl and told him of my predicament, hoping for a suggestion that would alleviate my suffering. All he said was, "Have your mom call me when she gets home."

I munched a Baby Ruth bar, careful to chew on the opposite side, and waited for mom. When she arrived, she called my uncle, then whisked me by cab to his office in Queens. The leaves were changing, becoming a deep umber before turning red. Despite the chill, I was sweating as we pulled into his driveway.

Uncle Carl instructed me to get into a dental chair and wait while he finished with another patient. His face was somber and his manner brusque. I talked to Peggy who was helping her father.

"Your dad's in a bad mood," I said.

"He's that way every day. The only time he tries to smile is when he's working on a paying patient."

My uncle walked in and barked at Peggy. "Ipish, get me a tray."

Uncle Carl stood over me and looked in my mouth. All I could see of him was his thin face highlighted by a Hitler-like moustache, and fingers studded with calluses. He pushed a dental X-ray against my throbbing tooth and held it with his index finger while Peggy pushed the button on the X-ray machine.

He developed the film, and when he came back, he said, "You have a nasty cavity we need to fill."

Before I could say anything, he drilled into my tooth without giving me an injection to prevent pain. "Ow, that hurts!" I yelled.

"It will be faster this way and it will only take me a few minutes."

My mother held my hand and I squeezed every time the drill hit a nerve ending. I thought the pain of having the cavity filled was worse than the throbbing I had been experiencing. When Carl was finished my eyes were blurry with tears.

Carl turned to my mother. "He'll be okay now. If he has any pain give him a couple of aspirins."

Carl moved into the next room without hugging me or giving my mom, his sister, a kiss. I stared after him in disbelief. All Peggy could do was shrug. "Feel better," she said.

My mother whisked me into a cab for the trip home. I rested my head on her shoulder while holding my hand to my cheek. I wondered why Leo, or anybody, had to be or would want to be a professional like Carl

As I pulled into the parking lot of the hospital, I thought, no wonder Peggy turned out chronically unhappy and morose, having that kind of a father in her formative years. I sat in the waiting room waiting for Peggy's surgeon, a friend of mine, to bring me news. Peggy's son was out tending to his lawn maintenance business and her daughters, I thought, must be with their father who was at home with terminal pancreatic cancer. Peggy could never get a break. I was hoping that it would be different this time—that there was some innocuous reason for her bloating and abdominal discomfort. In my mind, though, I was thinking the worst. A television droned in the background and sullen people stared at the images, lost in thought, hoping like me, for a benign outcome for their loved ones.

I saw Peggy's surgeon come into the room, and by his somber face and defeatist posture, knew the news wasn't good.

"How is she, Ed?" I said.

He shook his head. "I'm sorry. All we did was open and close. Her whole abdomen is filled with cancer—ovarian cancer. There's really nothing to do but keep her comfortable and make whatever time she has left as pleasant as possible.

I buried my face in my hands and cried.

From our bed, Dotty called out. "Are you okay? You screamed."

My glazed eyes opened wide. "Just a bad dream."

"Want to talk about it."

"Not really. Just goblins and ghosts."

She smiled. "Yeah, sure."

"I think I'll call pathology. I know the head of the department. Maybe we can get the results of the tests on your lymph nodes."

I went into the kitchen, took a swig of diet coke, and rubbed an ice cube from the glass on my forehead. My finger trembled as I dialed. After exchanging a few pleasantries with the chief pathologist, I asked if he had the results. "I didn't realize it was your wife," he said. "We're signing them all out as negative."

"Thank God," I said.

"But because it's your wife, I'm going to do the new radio-immune fluorescent technique we've developed. It'll pick up cancer cells even when the regular pathology is negative."

"Will that help in staging the cancer?"

"No, that's based on standard pathology. We don't have enough experience with this modality to make it clinically useful as yet. But I'm definitely going to do it. Call me tomorrow."

Before I could say anything, he hung up. I thought, if this new technique is of no clinical use, why am I letting him do it? All I'll do is worry if it detects anything. Then again, if it's normal, I'll feel a hell of a lot better. My head was caught in a vise with a carpenter cranking the handle, narrowing the distance between the walls.

I went back to the bedroom and told Dotty what was happening. "That's good news," she said. "Right?"

"I'll feel even better if that new technique is negative. We'll know tomorrow." I walked over to Dotty, stooped over and kissed her forehead. "Let's think positive. The good news is that your breast cancer stage is a 2A, Two because it was between 2 and 5 centimeters in size and A because there was no lymph node involvement. All your markers were normal. With that stage and negative markers you've been told your prognosis is excellent—eighty-five to ninety percent five-year survival. And you know I'd never bet on a ten to one shot, so you're going to be fine."

Dotty pointed to the ceiling. "From your mouth to His ears."

"Do you want to play ghost or super ghost?" I asked.

"No, I'm tired. Besides, you never win."

"Just try me."

"Another time."

Dotty and I were both exhausted, and as her eyes closed, so did mine. Images of Peggy re-occupied my mind.

* * *

I didn't want to be the one to tell Peggy, so like a coward I waited until after she had spoken to Ed to go in and visit that evening. "You know?" she asked.

I nodded.

"This really sucks." she said. "But my whole life has been like this. When I think of all the times I thought about suicide, I guess this is poetic justice."

I expected to feel bad, but why did I feel guilty? Was it because we lived so close to each other and I hadn't seen enough of her over the years? After all, I had been good to her. I had lent her money on numerous occasions and she hadn't repaid any of it. Maybe I felt guilty because I hadn't given her the organ in my house that she coveted. I had no use for it, since after taking lessons, it was apparent that I lacked one iota of musical ability. At least I could rectify that oversight now.

I leaned over and kissed Peggy on the forehead. "We'll still have plenty of time to talk, and I want to listen to you play the organ I'm sending over to your house."

She smiled. "Thank you, and we do need to talk. I want to share some secrets about our family that I only recently discovered."

More family secrets. First Dotty's aunt and now this. Whatever this is. "We'll talk when you get home."

Three days later, she was discharged and hospice care was arranged for her and her husband at their home. True to my word, I arranged to have the organ delivered to her. I visited often and listened to her play. One day, while her husband was napping, she said, "Let's talk."

"About what?"

"You know when my dad passed away a few years ago, they said it was a heart attack?"

I nodded.

"It wasn't. He overdosed on Percocet."

"He never was very happy," I said. "So what difference does it make?"

Peggy shook her head. "None really. But what does make a difference is what I found out going through his things."

"What?"

Peggy wiped her forehead and slumped in her chair. She took a sip of water and swallowed hard. "I have a sister."

"You have a what?"

"It seems before I was born, they had a Down Syndrome baby. My parents institutionalized the infant right away. They've been supporting her all along. I was going to track her down before I got sick, but never got around to it. She's probably dead since there were no records of payments for several years before my father died. Will you help me find out for sure?"

I nodded. "Of course, but why all the secrecy."

"Damned if I know. I'm so angry. I was essentially deprived of a father and he continued the deprivation by keeping me from ever knowing my only sibling. But you know how selfish my father was. It was all about him."

Peggy grabbed her chest and slumped further into her chair. "I'm so tired," she said. "Help me into bed."

She leaned on me, as we walked into the bedroom. I wished I had let her lean on me more when her health was good.

Peggy and her husband passed away several weeks later, only a few days apart. I had managed to ascertain her sister, also my cousin, had preceded her into the grave by a few years. As I stood at Peggy's funeral, watching her casket being lowered into the ground, I couldn't help wonder what all this secrecy was about. Who was protecting who from what?

When the doorbell rang, I shook my head to loosen the cobwebs. It was my brother and his wife followed in short order by two close friends. We sat in the living room reminiscing about our children. I told the story of my daughter when she was three. We used to go to a community pool to cool off from the blazing heat of the Florida summer. I'd be in the pool and my daughter would stand on the edge wiggling her tush.

"Come on, Ruth," I said. "Do a two and a half with a twist in the pike position."

She'd stand there and wiggle, looking around to see if she had garnered any attention. She bent her knees and kept shaking her hips, as if she were trying to contemplate the dive in her mind.

"I know you can do it. Let's see that two and a half with a twist in the pike position."

By this time, everyone around the pool had there gazes focused on Ruth. After what seemed like an interminable wait, she smiled, gave one last wiggle, and jumped into my arms.

Hearing that story made everyone laugh. Even Dotty managed a smile. It was supper time, so I called in a takeout order of various types of pizza. I knew Dotty wouldn't eat anything, as her stomach knotted when she was tense. This caused her to lose her appetite.

After everyone had eaten and left, Dotty was still fiddling with most of her first slice. "I'm scared," she said.

"I know." All I could think of to add was a paraphrasing of a song from *Gypsy*. "Wherever we go, whatever we do, we'll do it together." We stood in the kitchen holding on to each other.

The next day, I procrastinated about calling the pathologist. I wasn't sure I could handle more bad news and in this case, I wasn't sure what a positive result on this new test would have meant. I put on a pair of shorts and sneakers, and rode my stationary bike until sweat poured off me. I was hoping to achieve an endorphin high, but at the conclusion of my ride, the knots in my stomach were unchanged. I fiddled with a bowl of Honey Nut Cheerios and raspberries.

Dotty came into the kitchen. Her hand gravitated toward her missing breast. "Did you call yet?"

I shook my head. "I'll call in a little while. I want to make sure they're finished and have the results."

Later, when Dotty had reminded me for the third time, I picked up the phone and dialed. My finger trembled as I pushed each button. "Memorial Hospital, calls may be monitored for quality assurance. How can I help you?"

"This is Dr. Winick. I'd like the pathology department please."

> *"You have reached the surgical Pathology Department. Listen carefully as our prompts have changed. If you want a report, press one."*

Here we go again. I rocked back and forth. *"If you want to speak to a pathologist, Press two."*

I jabbed two with my right middle finger. A sing song recording answered. *"Hold the line, please. Someone will be with you in a moment."*

I shifted my weight from foot to foot. My feet ached by the time I spoke to a live person. "Can I help you?" she asked.

"This is Dr. Winick. I'd like to speak to Dr. Gerber, please."

After several minutes, he got on the phone. "I have good news. Even with the new technique, there's no evidence of cancer in any of the lymph nodes."

I thanked him, as my body went limp. Small victory, I thought, but one surely needed. I raced into the bedroom to tell Dotty, and for the first time in weeks, she had a broad grin on her face.

"What now?" she asked.

"You have to see Dr. Sedgeway at the end of next week. Then we'll make an appointment with the oncologist and plastic surgeon.

Dotty's grin converted to a frown. "I'm not looking forward to any of that."

I walked over and hugged her. "I know. But as I said, we'll get through this together."

I thought of Peggy and her husband. I knew that breast cancer had a better prognosis than pancreatic or ovarian cancer, but cancer is cancer, and as such frightening. All I could do was hope Dotty's outcome would be different from my cousin's.

Chapter Six

–Smiles

Shortly after Dotty was diagnosed with breast cancer and had recovered from her mastectomy, I received Sherri's letter and invitation to her twentieth. I could visualize her ever-smiling, pale face, dotted with broken blood vessels. I was scared that the chemotherapy Dotty would have to undergo would cause her blood vessels to burst and leave her prone to more serious bleeding. I thought back to when Sherri and I had met in my pediatric office.

Sherri had brought her newborn, Vicki, to see me. The infant had been full term, but only weighed three pounds and a few ounces at birth. As I took the history, I wondered how Sherri maintained a constant smile. She was nineteen, unmarried, and the baby's father was in jail. Perhaps she didn't realize the daunting task ahead of her—perhaps she was in denial? When she told me about her recently diagnosed medical condition, my lips quivered, but her smile remained fixed. She related to me that she was being taken care of at the University of Miami Medical School, by a hematologist, for a life threatening vascular condition called thrombotic thrombocytopenic purpura, a disease that ate her platelets causing bruising and potentially more serious bleeding. She needed to have a transfusion of plasma every three weeks in order to survive. How could she be so upbeat—so happy? As I got to know her, I realized this wasn't an act. She remained positive despite what life had in store. I knew in her position, I would be devastated, and wouldn't respond like she did.

"How will you be able to handle things?" I asked.

"My mother's going to help. I have medical insurance through the state. I have a part-time job to supplement what the government gives us." She looked at Vicki and smiled. "We'll be okay."

I nodded despite wanting to shake my head in disbelief. After examining the baby, I told her to increase the feedings as Vicki hadn't gained enough weight. "Come back in two weeks," I said. "So we can weigh the baby."

Sherri smiled and nodded.

Two weeks later she returned. When I told her Vicki still wasn't thriving, I expected her to become sullen. Instead, she said, "The baby's eating fine. What could be wrong? What do we have to do to find out?"

I admired her upbeat attitude—let's find out what's wrong and fix it. I outlined the preliminary tests Vicki would have to undergo. "Let's do them as soon as possible," Sherri said.

We ran a number of blood and X-ray studies that didn't reveal the cause for Vicki's failure to thrive. I told Sherri we would need to get more extensive testing if the baby continued not to gain weight at the proper rate. I explained that in this type of situation, any organ system could be involved. The trick is to find out which one by doing as few invasive tests as possible.

She smiled. "I have faith in you."

At least someone does, I thought. I knew how often the evaluation for failure to thrive proved fruitless.

Over the next few months, Vicki grew appropriately for height and even gained weight, albeit at a slower rate than I would have liked. When six months had passed, my concern heightened as the baby had fallen off the low weight curve she had been maintaining. I decided it was time for more complex testing. When I told Sherri, she looked on the bright side. "It can't be too bad," she said. "Look how great Vicki's developing. She's turning over both ways."

I nodded. "That is great. But we still need to find out why she isn't gaining enough weight. Even though we haven't been able to document a urinary infection, the kidneys are the most likely system that would cause this problem. Let's get a bunch more cultures and if she is having infections then we'll need to treat her and get some fancy X-rays of the bladder and kidneys." I outlined to her the studies that would be needed.

She nodded. "Let's do it."

After the third or fourth culture finally revealed an infection, I treated Vicki and scheduled the tests. They revealed moderate enlargement of the kidneys because when she voided some of the urine refluxed back up to the kidneys. This was the reason she was having intermittent infections, and I hoped it was also causing her failure to thrive.

"We can take care of it," Sherri said. "Can't we?"

I nodded. "I'm going to send her to a pediatric urologist. Vicki's reflux is severe enough that he might want to operate to prevent further kidney damage. He'll explain the whole procedure to you."

"I knew you'd find the problem."

Why did it take me so long, I thought? I did plenty of negative urine cultures. Maybe I should have done more. I hoped this was the cause of Vicki's failure to thrive. If not, I was at a complete loss. "Let's see what the urologist says."

The urologist concurred with me, explained everything to Sherri and scheduled the operation. When she came to me the day before surgery to have Vicki cleared medically, she was smiling. "I know this is going to work."

I winked, lifted my hand and crossed my fingers. "I hope so."

"It will. You'll see."

Sherri proved to be a good prognosticator. After the surgery, Vicki remained uninfected and thrived. She made up for lost time by gaining weight rapidly. There was no arguing that Sherri's upbeat attitude had been validated.

Over the next two years things continued to go well. Vicki was thriving and Sherri continued getting plasma every three weeks with no untoward effects. One day, Sherri came into the office. An ear to ear grin was plastered on her face. "I'm getting married," she said.

"Good for you."

"He's a great guy—so understanding about my problem. We want to have children right away."

I hope they'll be healthier than Vicki as a baby, I thought. I gave her a hug. "Nothing but the best for you."

I went back to reading Sherri's letter. "We Devers are a peculiar lot," she wrote. She reminded me of the illnesses of her next two children that mimicked her own disease. They too involved an inflammation of the blood vessels, and like her malady was life-threatening—like Dotty's breast cancer, life-threatening.

*   *   *

Two years later, Sherri brought her second baby girl to see me. This one was full term and full weight, seven pounds two ounces. With each visit, when I told Sherri how well the blond haired baby with her mother's dimples was doing, Sherri's perennial grin broadened. Everything progressed normally until the little girl was three-years-old.

One day, Sherri brought Donna into the office. She was concerned about a rash that had started around Donna's buttocks and the back of her thighs and spread to other parts of her body. She told me that Donna was having severe abdominal pain. My God, I thought. She's black and blue, bruised all over. Abuse crossed my mind, but I doubted it. The clinical picture was classic for H-S purpura, an inflammation of the vascular system, but not as serious as Sherri's condition. How to explain this to Sherri?

"What's wrong?" she asked.

I outlined my suspicion to her—about how the bruising was caused by a fragile vascular system, not a low platelet count—that the cause really wasn't known, but was thought to have an allergic basis. "Everything should be okay if. . . ."

"If what?"

"If Donna doesn't develop kidney problems."

"You mean like Vicki?"

I shook my head. "On rare occasion, perhaps one in twenty, progressive kidney damage can occur leading to kidney failure. We'll keep a close eye on Donna." What I didn't say was that this could happen despite any medical treatment I might provide.

"I'm sure you'll watch carefully."

"The good news is that the rest of what she has, the bruising, and the abdominal pain, will be gone in a few weeks."

"Good!" Sherri said. "I'm sure you won't let that kidney business happen and Donna will be fine."

I wish I had such optimism, and didn't want to dampen it by telling her it was out of my control. I hope her prognostication would again be accurate. "You'll need to bring Donna back every week or two so that we can follow her urinary findings and kidney function. You know you can call me anytime in between if there's anything that bothers you."

She smiled. "I know."

I followed Donna cautiously over the next six months. After two weeks, her abdominal pain was gone, the bruising had faded and all her blood and urine parameters remained normal. At six months, nothing had changed, no kidney problems had developed. I told Sherri we could stop holding our breath. "The illness is over and Donna won't have any adverse effects."

Sherri's grin widened revealing the same dimples as Donna. "I was sure of that all along."

I continued reading Sherri's letter. She seemed happy and as always, remained in good spirits. Her disease was well controlled requiring a plasma transfusion now only every six weeks. She was sure there would be a medical breakthrough that would enable her to live without transfusions. Typical of her, always optimistic, I thought. I hoped there would be a similar breakthrough in breast cancer that would enhance Dotty's chance of survival. As I read on, I thought about Sherri's third child and how sick she had been.

After I informed Sherri that Donna no longer was in danger of kidney disease, she told me she was pregnant and once again looking forward to motherhood. I returned her broad grin. I was hoping this child would be free of any medical catastrophe.

As if reading my mind, she said, "I know we're not going to have any problems with this baby."

I put my crossed fingers into the air, and walked over to give her a hug. "I sure hope you're right. You deserve it."

Six months later, Sherri gave birth to her third daughter, Dana. She was full term, full weight, free of deformities and the tintype of her mother. When I told Sherri, her grin broadened. "She is beautiful, and best of all, she's perfect."

"You bet," I said.

For the first four years of her life, Dana thrived, developing normally, and without serious illness. Sherri's other children were doing well too, and she herself was improving, requiring transfusions only every four to six weeks. It looked like Sherri would finally get a break from the constant threat of serious medical illness that hovered over her family. Frankly, I couldn't believe that she maintained her smile and optimism all these years.

One day, Sherri brought Dana into the office with a high fever. Just a routine illness, I thought. I took great care in examining Dana, and finding nothing adverse, I told Sherri that it was probably just a viral illness that would resolve in a few days.

Sherri smiled. "I hope so."

Three days later, now five days into the illness, Dana's fever still raged. I reexamined her, and this time, much to my dismay, there were abnormal physical findings. Dana had several lymph nodes in her neck. One was an inch long. She had reddened eyes without a discharge, an infected throat, a faint rash on her body, and some slight peeling of her fingers. My God, I thought, she has Kawasaki's disease. It's so rare, though. I had trouble believing this was true, as I had never seen a case before.

When I told Sherri, she furled her brow, all the while maintaining her smile. "Sounds like a motorcycle not a disease."

"It does, doesn't it?" Before she asked, I told her that this could be a serious condition like Donna's and hers—that this too was a vasculitis, an inflammation of the blood vessels like theirs.

Sherri's smile lessened and she stared at me, as if waiting for me to deliver the bad news about this condition. "What can we expect with this one?" she said. "What caused it?"

"We have no idea about the cause, and thus have no definite tests to run to prove the diagnosis. Unlike your illness, the platelets usually go up in the second week of the disease. The good news is that it's a self limiting disease that usually burns itself out in a few weeks. However, she'll have to be hospitalized until then."

Again Sherri's eyes bore into me. "Okay, so what's the bad news?"

I took a deep breath. "Occasionally the inflammation involves the coronary arteries and causes an aneurysm, a weakening in the walls of those vessels." I explained all the ramifications of this including all the dire consequences if an aneurysm should rupture.

"How often does that happen?" she asked.

"Somewhere in the range of twenty percent."

"How are we going to treat this so it won't happen?"

"I'm going to put her on high dose aspirin therapy to cut down the inflammation." What I felt guilty about not saying was that I had recently read an article about the use of immunoglobulins in the treatment of Kawasaki's disease. The report was from several foreign countries and was quite encouraging, but as yet had not been approved for use in the United States and therefore I couldn't use it. I didn't want to give false hope for treatment not available to me. "We'll have to do a lot of echocardiograms over the next few months to monitor Dana for the development of a coronary aneurysm."

Typical of Sherri, she smiled and shook her head. "Not going to happen," she said.

After I admitted Dana, I sat in my office calling colleagues, asking if they ever heard of the combination of illnesses that afflicted the Dever family. The answer was a uniform no. That evening when I went to visit Dana, I stopped in the library to search the medical literature. I couldn't find any similar constellation of diseases in the same family. I walked toward Dana's room shaking my head.

Dana's initial echocardiogram was normal. "I told you," Sherri said.

"Remember though," I said. "An aneurysm can develop later."

She nodded. "It won't."

Again Sherri proved prophetic. One week later Dana's fever was gone and her echocardiogram was still normal. I sent her home on high dose aspirin to be continued for a prolonged period of time. Every month we repeated the echocardiogram and every month it was normal. After the six-month check, I told Sherri everything would be okay. "A coronary aneurysm doesn't develop after six months."

Sherri's perennial grin broadened reminding me of the proverbial Cheshire cat. "I was sure everything was going to be okay."

"I guess you were right." I walked over and hugged her. "No more of this nonsense, okay?"

"Okay, for sure. I'm even doing better."

I finished reading Sherri's letter and remembered the tribulations. I could see why she had dubbed the Dever clan a peculiar lot. I then picked up the invitation inviting me to the twentieth anniversary party of her surviving thrombotic thrombocytopenic purpura. I smiled, and hoped that if Dotty and I could keep a positive outlook like Sherri, Dotty would have a similar outcome. We too would be able to celebrate Dotty's twentieth anniversary of survival from breast cancer.

Chapter Seven

–Tommy

The following week, I went with Dotty to see Dr. Sedgeway. Every chair in the office was crammed with women and an occasional man, one more sullen than the other. We flipped through magazine after magazine, staring at pictures without reading a word, waiting for Dotty's name to be called. After over an hour, we were ushered into the examining room. Dr. Sedgeway breezed in, greeted us, and focused his pale blue eyes on Dotty. "So, how do you feel?"

Some discomfort," she answered. "But otherwise okay."

"Let's have a look." He opened Dotty's paper gown and with his fingers palpated the area of the surgical incision. "It looks perfect. My assistant is going to remove the drain and take out the stitches. Keep the dressing on another week. Come back and let me take another look in a month. Don't forget to set up those appointments with Dr. Wayling and the plastic surgeon.

I hoped Dr. Wayling would be more caring than a lot of physicians, including me at times. I remembered Tommy."

Dr. Sedgeway got off his stool, walked to the door and turned his head. "I'm glad it turned out so well."

How could it have turned out so well, I thought? She has breast cancer. How could that be good? "Everything seems to be going well," I said.

"Yeah, right, very well," Dotty said.

I put my arm around Dotty as we walked to the car. "Up to going out for lunch?"

"I'm tired," Dotty said. "Let's just go home."

After nibbling a piece of string cheese, Dotty excused herself to take a nap. I sat at the kitchen table scarfing down my second bagel smeared with orange marmalade. Solving the crossword puzzle was proving difficult, since my mind was wandering. What is an eleven-letter word that means reliving the past? I closed my eyes trying to conjure up the answer. Of course, I began reminiscing. The movie in my mind started, and Tommy was starring.

I walked into Tommy's room. The smell of disinfectant wafted through the air. He was sitting Indian style on the sterile sheets of his hospital bed, wiping away a tear that had run down his freckled face. How are you doing, champ?" I asked."

"Talk to me damn it! Tell me what's going to happen. I need to know. Do I have cancer?"

"The bone marrow shows some hyperplastic cells. We won't know if there are neoplastic components until the pathologist reviews the slides." What am I saying to a twelve-year-old?

"Stop with the doctor talk. I'm twelve-years-old. I have a right to know."

"Maybe we should talk when your parents are here, after we get your test results. Just hang in there, champ."

"That's the trouble. My parents are always around. They just went to get some coffee. They never leave me alone. They treat me like a baby, just like you do. I have cancer, don't I?"

I felt bad that I hadn't taken more time with Tommy to try and relieve his apprehension. I knew I was in a hurry to get to my son's Little League game. It was the last game of the season—the one that would determine the league championship. My son was the star first baseman and I promised my wife and him that I'd be there on time. I made a decision to stay with Tommy at least until his parents returned, even though I knew I couldn't answer his question.

As I took my time making this choice, Tommy stood up on his bed. "Will someone please talk to me? I feel like there's nobody around to hear me. All day today I couldn't stop thinking about a fly I saw walking on the ceiling. I imagined it getting caught in flypaper. Its wings made a hissing noise that stopped when the flapping stopped. I keep thinking is this going to happen to me? I hope not. I have too much to do."

I put my arms around him and hugged, trying to be reassuring. "Tommy, it's too early to know for sure. We really have to wait until we get the results. We'll have them tomorrow."

"Doc, when I look at myself in the mirror, I see bruises all over my body. This greenish-yellow spot on my leg happened when I slid into second base." He ran his hand across the purple area on his right cheek. "That's where Jamie tagged me. I have no idea where the Hell this bruise on my stomach came from. All these bruises must be cancer. I overheard you tell my parents that the bone marrow was to make sure I didn't have leukemia."

"That true, Tommy, but let's stay cool till we know. Even if it is leukemia, most children can be completely cured. You can't let yourself get down."

He shook as I held him in my arms. When he had calmed down, I excused myself to go to the bathroom. I picked up the bathroom phone to call Dotty, to tell her I'd be late for the game. Tommy was already on the phone with his friend Jamie. I eavesdropped on their conversation.

"What's up, Tommy my man?" Jamie asked.

"That Goddamn doctor won't tell me anything, and I thought he was my buddy. He treats me like a baby, just like my folks. I've got a right to know what's happening with my own body."

"What's wrong with you?"

"I think I have leukemia. I'm bruised all over. They stuck this huge needle into my hip bone and now no one will tell me what's wrong. The Doc just gives me some medical mumbo-jumbo and my parents think I'm five-years-old."

"The Hell with them, Tommy. You've got to get well. We have the championship game next week. If we beat the Orioles, we'll be champs. We need you to pitch. I'm sure you're gonna be okay."

"I'm scared, Jamie. I can't think about pitching. If they would only talk to me, I'd feel a lot better."

"Hang in there. Remember what Yogi said. It ain't over until it's over. You know these docs and your parents worry about everything. If they don't give you the word soon, tell them your buddy Jamie, will clean their clocks. Feel better. I'll see you tomorrow."

I opened my eyes and stared at the puzzle that was almost entirely blank. It felt a little like my life. I went back to the bedroom and lay down next to Dotty.

Several days later, Dotty was apprehensive as she got ready for her appointment with Dr. Wayling. She fussed with her hair, going back and forth between brush and curling iron. "Damn, I can't get my hair to lie straight."

"You look fine. Besides, you should be grateful you're not missing hair like me."

"That's not going to last much longer."

"I'm sorry. I didn't mean to say that."

"Don't be," she said. "You have a full head of hair."

"Right, creative combing."

Dotty smiled, but continued fussing with her hair. I wondered if she looked at this as the last hurrah before the rigors of chemotherapy. "You better hurry," I said. "Or we'll be late for your appointment."

"Big deal. I don't want to hear what he has to say anyway."

"I know, but chemotherapy is a necessary evil to bear in order to achieve our goal—the same goal that really is the mantra of our Jewish faith, survival."

Dotty stared at me, as tears welled in her eyes. "I know."

We hugged. "Now get ready."

She nodded.

When we reached Dr. Wayling's office, the sight of pale women, sitting with baseball hats or pink scarves covering their bald heads, caused me to shiver. I could only imagine how Dotty felt. I guessed that's why she spent so much time with her hair before we left home.

We filled out reams of forms detailing clinical and insurance information. Then we waited until they made up a chart for Dotty. By the time we were called, the waiting room was almost empty. In that instance, the wait was a relief, since I no longer had to look at sickly women. I knew this was a defense mechanism to keep me from thinking this soon would be Dotty. I watched her turn pages while her gaze was focused on the front desk. I assumed that she was looking beyond being called back to what Dr. Wayling would have to say.

When at last we were ushered into his office, he was waiting. He was a hawkish looking man with a yarmulke on his head. I had known him since I had helped care for his children. After a cursory hello and a handshake, he got right down to business.

"Before we discuss chemotherapy," he said. "Give me a little background about your cancer. I have Dr. Sedgeway's report, but I'd like to hear it from you."

Good start, I thought. Let the patient talk. Listen to her. Let her express her fears and validate them.

Dotty spent about five minutes giving him a synopsis of her clinical course. "So what do you think?" she said. "Do I need chemotherapy?"

"Of course, no choice. Let me tell you what I think. There are two forms of therapy. The harsh form, consisting of cytoxan and adriamycin, and the more mild form of cytoxan, methotrexate and 5FU. In your case, I would only consider the more aggressive treatment."

"Why?" Dotty asked.

"Because of the size of your tumor. It will give you the best chance to avoid a recurrence."

Dotty's face became ashen and she shifted her position in the chair. I leaned forward, and grasped the edge of the desk.

"Let me tell you the regimen and side effects you might experience."

"Do I really need it—the harsh treatment?" Dotty asked.

"Yes you do. There's no other good option."

He then began to drone on about hair loss, bone marrow suppression, anemia, bleeding tendencies, risks of infection, cardiac complications, etc. Dotty shook her head, but he continued with his dissertation. It was obvious he had lost her and wasn't responding to her needs—to be involved in the decision making process. He sounded like a well-rehearsed automaton whose spiel smacked of one size fits all. I'm sure it wasn't his intention, but I realized Dotty was uncomfortable and wouldn't be seeing him for chemotherapy.

As Dr. Wayling continued his monolog, I too tuned him out. I thought again about Tommy and the guilt I still felt over being insensitive to him.

I reentered the room at the same time as Tommy's parents. Tommy was sitting on the bed with his arms wrapped around himself. Tears ran down his cheeks. His mother put her arm around Tommy and squeezed. She rested her head on his shoulder and joined in the crying.

Tommy lifted his mother's chin. "What's wrong with me?"

His mother looked at me and shrugged. "Doctor Paul says we won't know for sure until we have the results of the bone marrow test."

"Do I have leukemia?"

His mother shrugged again. "We hope not. Let's wait to talk about this when we get the results."

"Why won't you give me any straight talk? You're always treating me like a baby. Like the time you wouldn't let me sleep over Jamie's house until you checked with his parents that they'd be home. You didn't believe me when I told you they would. All you would say is that we were too young to be by ourselves. As if I didn't know."

I felt sorry for Tommy, as I watched this interplay with his mother. He so much wanted to be treated like a grownup, but of course, had the mind set of a child. My heart was breaking, but there was little I could do, or was there? "Maybe I can call in a favor and push pathology into giving us an answer today."

Tommy's parents smiled. I picked up the phone on Tommy's night stand and thumbed through his baseball magazine while I waited for the pathologist to come on the line. "John could you do me a special favor and read Tommy Jackson's slides now? I know it's almost time for you to leave, but I have a really frightened family. I'd really appreciate it. I'll owe you." He agreed to stay and do it. The fact that I cared for his children made it difficult for him to say no. It would take about an hour, just long enough for me to miss my son's game.

I took Tommy's parents aside. "I wish I could be more encouraging, but I really don't know. My gut feeling is that he doesn't have leukemia, but . . . We'll know in about an hour."

Tommy's father said, "I know how scared he is. When I was a kid, I remember storming out of the house when my parents wouldn't tell me about my grandfather's illness. Maybe, we try to protect Tommy too much."

Tommy's mother nodded.

Maybe so," I said.

"Talk to me!" Tommy shouted.

"You're right champ," I said. "I'm sorry." I told him what the pathologist said, and that we soon would be able to answer all his questions. While we waited for him to call, Tommy related to us his dream from the night before.

"I dreamed of my grandfather's funeral. Everyone was standing around crying. I asked, where's grandpa?

"My parents answered, 'He's with God.'

"Am I going to be with God too? I know grandpa had leukemia. Doesn't anyone remember that?

"The next thing that happened, Doc, is that I was dreaming about my own funeral. I saw everyone standing around. The priest said, 'he has gone to be with God.'

"A lightening bolt filled the sky, lifting me toward heaven. On hands and knees, I tried climbing down, but I just kept going up. I woke up screaming, tell me, tell me."

Tommy's parents ran over and threw their arms around him. I picked up the phone when it rang and listened to the pathologist relate his findings. "Thanks," I said.

"Good news, Tommy. You don't have leukemia. You have idiopathic thrombocytopenic purpura."

"There you go again, Doc. What the Hell are you talking about. Speak English."

I smiled. "You're right, champ. I'm sorry. One of the clotting factors in your blood is low. That's what's causing the bruising. You'll get better. You're not going to be with God."

I expected a look of relief, instead beads of sweat formed on his forehead and his face turned red. He looked at his parents. "God Damn it! I'm twelve-years-old. It's about time you treated me like that." He got out of bed and ran into the lounge. We didn't follow.

I refocused on Dr. Wayling when he said, "That's pretty much it. Do you have any questions?"

Dotty shook her head. I was still thinking about Tommy, and reflexively answered. "I don't think so. We'll get back to you."

"We should start as soon as possible."

We'd been told time was not critical. A few weeks would make no difference. "I know," I answered. "We'll be in touch."

On the way home, Dotty was agitated. "There is no way I'm going to see that man. He sounded more like an orator than a doctor."

"I must admit that I had the same impression. I'm sure he's a good doctor. After all, he has a good reputation. But he just wasn't relating. We'll get a second opinion. I'll ask colleagues for a referral. Also, my brother has a friend in New York who's a nationally known oncologist. I'll ask his opinion about the two kinds of treatment, and find out if there's anyone down here you can use."

"Thanks for being so understanding."

"No thanks needed." I reached out and held her hand while I drove.

I realized that no form of chemotherapy would work unless Dotty had a kind, understanding doctor who would listen to her. I thought about Tommy. I wished I had come to that realization before putting him through all that emotional trauma.

Chapter Eight

—Aaron

I spoke to my brother's friend on a number of occasions. He was kind enough to review Dotty's clinical data. It was his opinion that the stronger chemotherapeutic regimen was inappropriate for Dotty, but ultimately that decision would be between Dotty and her treating oncologist. He supplied the name of two physicians in our area, who according to him, were caring and were up on the latest scientific advances.

The first oncologist we went to see was in Miami Beach. Sitting in his waiting room with pale women, whose heads were arrayed in a number of different coverings, from turbans to baseball hats, made me feel queasy again. Soon, this may be Dotty. I had to get over these negative feelings. When we were called into the doctor's office, he was affable enough, but I could sense by Dotty's behavior, like clearing her throat, and shifting positions in her chair, that she wasn't comfortable. At least he confirmed that the milder chemotherapy was appropriate for her. Although I knew better, I couldn't help thinking that cancer is cancer, and chemotherapy is chemotherapy. I was sensitized by cancer patients I had taken care of, particularly Aaron.

In the car on the way home, Dotty didn't talk until we were halfway there. "He was okay," she said. "But I wasn't entirely comfortable. What do you think?"

"The same. He sounded competent enough, but he wasn't personality plus."

"It was more than that. He seemed to talk around my questions rather than responding directly to them."

"I understand what you're saying. We have an appointment in Aventura with Dr. Orgel in two days. Let's see how you feel about him. If that doesn't work out, there are more fish in the sea. You've been told delaying chemotherapy a few weeks isn't going to make a difference. So let's see what happens."

We pulled into the driveway, and when I stopped the car and shut off the engine, Dotty threw her arms around me. "Thanks for being there for me."

"No thanks needed."

After we had a bite of lunch, Dotty excused herself to take a nap. I was agitated and unable to concentrate on a Shakespearean play I was rereading, *Loves, Labors, Lost.* So I sprawled on the couch to watch test patterns on TV. Only insipid soap operas were on, and the incessant whining of the characters, caused my eyes to flutter shut. The movie in my mind started up and Aaron was on center stage.

I met Aaron and his mother Rachel for the first time in the early seventies, when she came to interview me as a potential pediatrician for her son. They had just moved to South Florida and had been given my name by a northern colleague.

Aaron streaked into the office and headed straight for a chess set on my desk. He had a mop of curly blond hair and an impish smile. He looked at me as he fingered the pieces, trying to see if I would protest.

"Do you play?" I asked.

He smiled. "My daddy taught me. I'm pretty good."

"Would you like to play?"

He nodded. After several moves, I allowed myself to get trapped into a fool's mate—a mate that only requires four moves.

"I got you," he chortled.

"You're much too good for me," I said.

Rachel grinned. "You do very well with him," she said. "But I need a pediatrician who will listen to me. Mothers know their child best, and I know my child better than anyone."

She's very pushy, I thought. But I had worked with many difficult mothers. In fact, if truth be told, I found it a challenge. I took a close look at Rachel before responding. She was wafer thin, with a large nose and long, straggly brown hair. She wore a shapeless sack covering her stick figure, and hadn't applied makeup, leaving her complexion almost ghostlike.

"I'll be happy to listen to you. I've even been told I'm good at it."

She smiled at me. "I think we're going to do fine together." She handed me a folder. "These are Aaron's records from up north."

Rachel eyed me as I read. I felt a rush of warmth on my face. I looked at Aaron who was moving chess pieces around the board and was scolding the white knight for allowing himself to be trapped.

I turned to Rachel and must have looked quizzical. "That's right." she said. "Aaron has leukemia. He's in remission, but is still on chemotherapy. We've been lucky. So far so good. He hasn't even lost any hair. I'm seeing an oncologist down at the University of Miami. He's continuing the protocol they started up north."

I was flabbergasted. He looked so well. "I, I'd be happy to take care of Aaron. I have several patients who have leukemia. If any problem comes up, you can call me anytime."

"Sometimes, I have trouble communicating with the oncologist, but he's the only show in town. I know you teach at the university. I might need you to intercede. Is that okay?"

I didn't know what she meant by intercede. "I know the people down there very well. I'm always willing to talk to them."

I guess my response, which was evasive, placated her. She asked me to be Aaron's pediatrician. I made an appointment to examine him after I had a chance to fully review his record.

Three weeks later, several days before our appointment, Rachel called. "Aaron's really sick," she said. "He has a high temperature."

I told her to bring Aaron right over. I knew that Aaron was on chemotherapy, which could suppress his immune system, making him more susceptible to serious infection.

Aaron came bouncing into the examining room. "He doesn't look very sick," I said.

"Looks can be deceiving. He's just not acting himself."

Even though he looked well and his physical exam was normal, I was concerned. "I really don't think there's anything seriously wrong, but because of his condition and his altered immunity, I think we should admit him, get a blood culture to look for a bacterial infection, and start him on IV antibiotics."

"No way I'm putting Aaron in the hospital. That's out of the question."

"Okay, why don't we get a blood count. If it's normal, we can get a blood culture, and give Aaron an injection of an antibiotic. In that case, I'd like to see him tomorrow, but please call me if you have any concerns at all."

As long as Aaron didn't have to be hospitalized, Rachel was happy with that approach. I was comfortable because I didn't think Aaron had anything seriously wrong. However, with him being immune suppressed, I couldn't be sure.

The next day, Aaron bounced into the office. He looked the same as the day before, except his cheeks weren't flushed. His fever was gone. "Let's play a game of chess," he said.

I had my secretary call for the blood culture results. When she handed it to me, I frowned.

"What's the matter?" Rachel asked.

"He has a bacterial infection in his blood stream. I can't believe it. He looked so well."

"I told you he was sick. He just wasn't his usual animated self. What do we do now?"

"Since he's better, we'll just keep him on antibiotics for ten days, and then repeat the blood culture. If there's any change call me."

Rachel was right. Mother knew best. Through the years I had learned to trust mothers' judgements, but as I was beginning to find out, Rachel's ability to detect subtle changes in her son was uncanny.

The blaring of a commercial awakened me. It was touting a woman could do it all, including cook up the bacon, and never let him forget he's a man. It was ironic this was the commercial that interrupted the movie in my mind.

As I was to learn later, Rachel was so multi-talented that she really could almost do it all. I checked on Dotty, and picked up a book to read, while I watched her sleep.

Several days later, we were in Dr. Orgel's office. We arrived at the end of his morning hours and the waiting room was empty. This put me somewhat at ease not having to stare at all those chemotherapy patients. After filling out the requisite paperwork, we were ushered into an office. We were greeted by his assistant, a perky young woman with a cherubic smile. She outlined the logistics of the office, and showed us the large room, sectioned by curtains, where the IV chemotherapy would be administered. There were comfortable lounge chairs for the patients that could be dropped into a totally reclined position. There was room for a family member like myself, to sit and hold their loved one's hand. The requisite IV poles were tucked into corners so as not to be obtrusive when not in use.

Back in the office, the assistant asked if there were any questions. She answered the general concerns about chemotherapy. How they would handle what I thought were the universal side effects of chemotherapy, such as the nausea and vomiting. She said many patients didn't experience this reaction, and if they did, there was medication to take before and during the ordeal that would lessen those side effects.

When Dotty asked specifics about the two different regimens we had been told about, the assistant smiled. "I think I'll let Dr. Orgel handle that one."

She took us into his office, and gave us a handout of his qualifications to read, while we waited. I was impressed by the over one hundred peer reviewed articles that he had published. Letters from grateful patients abounded. There were many diplomas and accolades on the wall. These were framed by pictures of him with celebrities at various fund-raising functions. Not much to look at, I thought—short, big nose—but what better way to show the passion for your field than being an advocate for your cause. I was prepared to like him, and hoped Dotty had the same reaction. I knew that she had come to the meeting with a positive perspective, as her friend, who was being treated by him for breast cancer, was effusive with her praise.

When he walked into the room, he put us instantly at ease. "I don't have a lot of questions," he said. I've reviewed all your records so I'm pretty familiar with your case. My assistant tells me you're concerned about which type of chemotherapy to pursue."

In unison, Dotty and I nodded.

"There's nothing to be gained from the harsher chemotherapy, and if you don't want any at all, that would be okay."

"Wouldn't that be unwise?" Dotty asked.

"If you choose to do nothing, your five year survival would be about sixty to sixty-five percent. I would recommend tamoxifen daily to shut off your estrogen. This alone would increase your five year survival to eighty-five percent." He paused to let us digest what he had said. "Do you have any questions so far?"

Dotty and I looked at each other, and I blurted out a question. "How much will chemotherapy improve her survival chances?"

"That's always the million-dollar question. In your wife's case, research has shown that the five year survival rate increases to approximately 95 percent.

He turned to Dotty. "The decision whether to have the chemo is strictly up to you. Of course, if you have any questions, I'll be happy to answer them."

Dotty leaned forward, putting her hands on his desk "If it were your wife, what would you do?"

He smiled. "If it were my wife, I would support any decision she made."

Dotty returned his smile and nodded. She asked a few questions about the specifics of the chemotherapy. She found out there would be six treatments, three weeks apart. She would need to have her blood monitored to make sure the chemotherapy didn't suppress her bone marrow too much, leaving her low in red cells, white cells and platelets. This could leave her anemic, in danger of infection, and prone to bleeding. Dr. Orgel assured her these side effects could be dealt with.

When Dotty had no further questions, he put his arm around her. "Give some thought to what we've talked about. If you have any questions, call me. Let me know what you decide."

When we left the office and were in the car, I could sense that Dotty's mood had elevated. "I like him," she said.

"I do too."

"What should I do?"

"Like Dr. Orgel said, I'll support any decision you make."

"The chemo does increase my survival chances by up to ten percent, doesn't it?"

I nodded.

"I want to survive, so I guess I have no choice. I'll have the chemo. My friend Harriet did, and look how well she's doing. I'll call Dr. Orgel and tell him. The sooner we get started, the sooner we'll finish, and hopefully this nightmare will end."

I realized that Dr. Orgel knew this would be her decision, but was smart enough not to make it for her. I wanted to reach out and hug Dotty, but as I was driving the car, I thought better of it. When we got home, Dotty went into the bedroom to let friends and family know what Dr. Orgel had said and what decision she had made.

I sat shaking at the kitchen table, staring into space. The movie in my mind, fast forwarded.

Several months later, Rachel and her husband invited my family to her sprawling ranch style home in Davie. Dotty thought it might be fun for our children to have the freedom to roam around and play with Aaron. I accepted Rachel's invitation.

She had a rambling house in an area of mini ranches. The property was surrounded by a rustic log fence. The house was encased by a beautiful arrangement of multicolored Impatiens interspersed with Sabal Palms. I pointed to the array. "That's beautiful."

Rachel smiled and waved her hand. "I planted all this myself."

The most impressive part of the interior of the house was a large baby grand piano that dwarfed the living room and the elaborate art work cluttering the walls.

I pointed to the piano. "Do you play?"

Rachel nodded, sat down, and played a Chopin interlude. I found myself repeating myself. "That's beautiful."

"I used to play professionally."

I looked around the room and stared at the walls filled with oils, etchings and watercolors. "That's an impressive collection," I said.

"Thank you. I created them all."

She's really one talented lady, I thought. Imagine being able to play the piano and paint like that. My art ability was confined to stick figures and my nonexistent musical talent was relegated to the role of listener only.

We walked outside and watched my seven-year-old son and five-year-old daughter frolic with Aaron in a game of hide and seek. Rachel went inside and emerged with a large SLR, 35MM, Pentax Camera. She took candid shots of the children immersed in their pleasures.

"I'd appreciate it if you would make a copy for me when you develop the film," I said.

She nodded and an impish grin broadened her face. "Of course I will."

The following week, Rachel stuck her head into my office and asked if I had a second. She handed me a package. "This is for you. I hope you like it."

I removed the brown wrapping paper to uncover two framed black and white photographs of my children. My daughter stood with her jaw jutting out and her pigtails flying. My son looked down pensively into a large bucket. Rachel had captured their essence.

"Thank you," I said.

"No, thank you," she said. "Thank you for taking such good care of Aaron and listening to me. I only give these gifts that I create to special people. They're real gifts of the heart."

I was touched by her generosity and thoughtfulness. I could have told her that she didn't have to give me a gift; it wasn't necessary. I realized, she would have just said it's something she wanted to do. I reached over, kissed her on the cheek, and thanked her again.

Several months later, Rachel barged into the office, unannounced, and dropped a stack of medical articles on my desk. "Have you seen these, Paul?" She asked.

I flipped through the articles. I was aware of the scientific data, but I hadn't read them all. "I know the recent data about central nervous system radiation and intrathecal methotrexate therapy increases the survival of leukemic patients, but Aaron's not eligible for the treatment. He's already on a protocol."

"That's where I need your help," she said. "The oncologist at the university turned me down. He said the same thing about protocols that you did. I need you to speak to him. I need you to . . ." She stopped and took a deep breath. "Please help me."

I agreed to help, but only if we get another expert opinion that this new therapy is appropriate for Aaron. I had a friend, Andy Grone, from my service days, who was now head of pediatric oncology at St. Jude's Hospital in Memphis, Tennessee. As a favor to me, he agreed to see Aaron. He concurred with Rachel that this treatment was appropriate for Aaron and might enhance his chance for a complete cure. He was even willing to have Aaron treated at St. Jude's, but because of the impracticality of the situation, Memphis being too far for the every day treatment Aaron would need, we decided to try and convince the oncologist at the university of Miami. Dr. Grone and I both called and cajoled him to give the new therapy locally. He was not happy, but he acquiesced to our pressure. He made Rachel aware of the rare but serious complications of the treatment. She was willing to take the risk to enhance Aaron's chances of survival.

Several months later, Aaron was in the midst of his new therapy. He finally had lost his hair and his body was lined with purple stripes marking the area that was being irradiated. His usual bounce was missing and his smiling face had a permanent frown. I hoped this treatment, at least, would turn out to be life saving.

I was pleased to see that after completion of the course of radiation, Aaron had regained his zest for life. He came to the office, ran to the chess set, finagled me into playing with him, and continued trapping me in the fool's mate.

"You always fall for my trick," Aaron said.

I smiled. "No, you're too good for me."

Rachel said, "He's back to his old self. I'm so happy, and more important, so hopeful for the future."

Aaron continued to take his standard chemotherapy, and his hair grew back Whenever I saw him in the office, he appeared to be his usual animated self. But to use a cliche, I was hoping the other shoe wouldn't drop.

Dotty's shaking me, interrupted the movie in my mind. "Are you okay?" she asked. "You're off in a dream world somewhere."

"You're right, I am. I'm dreaming of palm trees and hula skirts. We're going to stop in Hawaii, on our way to Australia and New Zealand when this is over. We're going to take that trip we cancelled. Just wait and see."

Dotty flung her arms around me and pointed to the ceiling. "From your mouth to His ears."

Several days later, Dotty started her treatment. Dr. Orgel had given her some Zofran to take the day before in an effort to mitigate any nausea or vomiting that might occur. We waited with other women who would also be ushered into the back room to have their chemotherapy. Most seemed relaxed, having gone through this before. The majority had their heads wrapped, but some preferred the bald look. They chatted between themselves. One woman, younger than Dotty smiled. "First time, I bet?"

Dotty nodded.

"I know it's frightening, but it's really not that bad. You'll see. It's like a family. We'll joke, talk about our family, about shows we've seen and books we've read. Anything to keep us from focusing on the cancer. We've become kind of a sisterhood." She looked at me. "Of course we get a little help from our friends." She turned back to Dotty. "My name is Liza with a Z, just like Liza Minelli." She scribbled her name and phone number on a piece of paper. "If you need someone to talk to, call me."

"Thank you," Dotty said. "You've put me at ease. At least as at ease as the situation allows."

We were ushered into the chemotherapy room. As we walked down the hall, I held Dotty's hand, while Liza put her arm around Dotty's shoulder. They were put in two chairs near each other. That's good, I thought. Maybe Dotty would have a friend who could help her through this ordeal. The nurse drew the curtain between them, and began to get Dotty ready. She jabbed her with a long needle, threaded a catheter into her vein, and attached the other end to an IV bottle. Then the nurse took a syringe filled with a yellow liquid to inject into the tubing.

Dotty withdrew her arm. "What's that?"

"More Zofran to prevent nausea and vomiting and to take the edge off. We have to put these medications in sequentially, one at a time, so you'll be here a few hours."

Dotty nodded, and the nurse injected the Zofran. Then, she hung a bag, bearing the first therapeutic agent, on the IV pole and piggybacked it into the running IV. She smiled. "You're going to do fine."

The nurse opened the curtain and I could see Liza was already getting her therapy. "Not too bad, ay?" she asked.

"So far so good. You're French Canadian?"

"You caught me. But I've been living in South Florida for over twenty years."

While I held Dotty's hand, the two women continued talking. "I'm going to be a grandmother for the second time," Dotty said. "My daughter's in New York. She's in her seventh month. I'm hoping to get up there for the birth, or at least for the bris if it's a boy."

"My daughter was just married," Liza said. I can't wait to be a grandmother."

After chatting like this for half an hour, the nurse switched IV bags of medication. So far so good, I thought. "Thanks for talking to me Liza," Dotty said. "It really distracted me. My eyes are closing though, and I'm not going to fight it."

"You shouldn't. We'll have plenty of time to talk some more."

I watched Dotty's eyelids tighten and after a few minutes there was a faint snore. Is she really that calm, I wondered, or is she just exhausted from not having slept the night before? Probably the latter. I closed my eyes and rubbed my temples. Then I opened them and scanned all the women in the room, eventually focusing on a wisp of a woman with a bald head. She looked childlike. Soon her face faded, only to be replaced by Aaron's.

One lazy summer day the office was unusually quiet, and I actually sat in my office, lights out, eyes closed, trying to take a nap. A knock on the door caused me to jump. My receptionist said, "Dr. Paul, Rachel and Aaron are up front. She doesn't have an appointment, but would really appreciate it if you could see her. She seems worried."

"Give me a few minutes to wash my face, then send her back."

Rachel was more haggard then usual. Her long hair was knotted and an old house dress hung on her. It was obvious she hadn't taken time for grooming. Aaron didn't look any different to me. What could Rachel be so worried about?

Paul, there's something really wrong," she said. "Aaron's responses are slow and he's becoming clumsy."

"Aaron," I said. "Would you like to play chess?"

He looked at me with a blank expression. When I pointed to the chess set, he walked over and moved a piece. There was something wrong. The knight doesn't move three squares ahead. Aaron knew that. He hadn't tried to get me into his usual fool's mate.

I asked Aaron to jump on the examining table so I could examine him. He only moved when I pointed, and he stumbled several times before struggling to lift himself onto the table.

"How long as he been like this?"

"Just a few days," Rachel said

I carefully examined Aaron, tapping him with a hammer to check his reflexes, sticking him with a pin to check sensation, making sure his cranial nerves were intact, and playing squeeze my hand and push on my hand with your foot. He was weak and had diminished response to the pin prick. His speech was slurred. I realized he had a neurological deficit and told it to Rachel. "It's either the result of his leukemia or a consequence of his treatment. I'm going to get a bunch of tests, then refer Aaron to a neurologist."

"Let's do it," she said. "The sooner we find out what's wrong, the sooner we'll be able to treat him and make him better."

After many specialty referrals and numerous diagnostic tests, it was apparent that Aaron's treatment had caused a severe condition called a demyelinating encephalopathy, which would cause Aaron to regress. Indeed, over time, Aaron's speech became more slurred then nonexistent. He lost control of his bodily functions and had to be put into diapers. His muscles shriveled and Rachel rigged a wagon to cart him around, as he could no longer walk.

I sat down many times with Rachel to explain the situation. "This condition is likely to progress before stabilizing," I said. "More than likely, Aaron won't improve. I'm so sorry, but there's nothing we can do."

She stared at me as she wiped her eyes. "You know I can never accept that."

One day, we sat in my office, and I tried to reinforce my prognosis, hoping to get her to accept Aaron's fate, and get on with her life. Rachel leaned forward and grasped my desk. Her knuckles turned white. "I'll never give up. At least, not until we've exhausted every possible treatment." She opened her purse and removed a number of articles that she tossed on my desk. "Are you familiar with these?"

I scanned the articles and realized they weren't from scientific journals, but from various holistic publications, and as such had no basis in fact.

As I read, Rachel stood. "Paul, I will take care of Aaron and love and cherish him no matter what the outcome, but I have to assure myself that nothing else can be done." She stared down at me for thirty seconds. Tears dripped from her eyes. "Will you help me?"

I realized if I took away her hope and continued to tell her nothing else could be done, she would have sought medical help elsewhere. I also knew these holistic treatments wouldn't harm Aaron. Besides. I felt guilty for my part in obtaining the aggressive therapy that he received. "You know you can count on me," I answered.

I didn't really understand the magnitude of the commitment I was making. Once a week, during lunch hours, Rachel would wheel Aaron into the office in his Red Flyer wagon. As I started the IV, Aaron would grimace and grunt, but would make no other protest. Megadoses of this vitamin or that mineral poured into his veins. Since the therapy was not medically approved, insurance would not reimburse me for my time and I provided the care gratis. I felt it was important to give Rachel hope, although in my heart I knew none existed.

At the beginning, Rachel remained positive, but as time dragged on and she saw no improvement in Aaron's condition, she slowly accepted the inevitability of the situation. Aaron's neurological status had stabilized, leaving him at an infantile level. He remained unable to control his bodily functions, unable to walk or talk, uttering only occasional groans. His wasted body resembled that of a shriveled, dying old man. My heart broke every time I looked at him, so I could only imagine how Rachel felt. Yet, she persisted in bringing him to the office for one IV potion or another.

My partners were not happy with the situation. They felt it took me away from paying patients, because of the time and energy expended. Dotty wasn't happy because these encounters left me emotionally drained.

After a year or so on these therapies, Rachel came to my office one day without Aaron. She was weepy eyed and angry. "Those doomsayer pundits, who said what we're doing wouldn't work, are right. Aaron's not getting better, but I appreciate everything you've done." She held up an etching of Einstein. "I was going to give this to you, but it's not good enough. I'm going to give it to my brother-in-law and sister-in-law instead. I'm doing a new one for you."

Two weeks later, she returned and presented me with a haunting etching of Einstein. My mouth filled with spittle, and I swallowed hard to clear my throat. What she had given me was unique, and part of her. She had created it for me as a labor of love. I was sure it would always remind me of Rachel and her tribulations. Einstein's eyes were wide and haunting. They followed me as I walked around the room to kiss Rachel's cheek. It was as if he was trying to impart his knowledge and humanity to me, so that I could understand the situation at hand.

The movie in my mind switched reels and forwarded twenty-five years. Aaron's condition was unchanged. He was still being cared for by Rachel. She and her husband adopted two Korean children. She was afraid to have any more of her own because of the high incidence of cancer in her family.

Rachel had become an activist for childhood cancer and had involved me. She was a founding member of the local chapter of Candlelighters, an advocacy group for children afflicted with cancer. I was a member and spoke many times at group functions. Through these efforts, I developed a practice with an inordinately high number of cancer patients. Caring for them often left me drained, but the euphoria I felt when a child survived made it all worthwhile. I just wish it had been Aaron. Rachel even testified before congress about the unique health needs of these children, constantly lobbying for more money to fund research projects.

In her spare time, she continued giving me gifts of the heart, including a ceramic rabbi resembling the Lladro statues that Dotty and I collected. The last gift that Rachel gave me was a ceramic plate with a blue Hebrew inscription, *Shalom Alechem.* In my heart, I sent the message back to her, *Alechem Shalom,* go in peace.

When my eyes blinked, the wisp of a woman who I had focused on was getting ready to leave. Dotty's eyes widened. "Is it over?" she asked.

I looked at the IV. "Almost," I said. "Just a little fluid left in the bag. Good to the last drop, you know."

She shook her head, as if trying to loosen the cobwebs. "I don't feel so bad."

"Are you complaining?"

She smiled. "Not in the slightest."

Liza was already finished and was preparing to leave. "If you need anything, or have any questions, give me a buzz."

"I really appreciate that."

"No problem. There were ladies here for me when I started. I know what help and support from people who have been there and done that can be, ay."

"Ay," Dotty said.

Liza smiled. "See you in three weeks, same place, same station. I only have two treatments left. By then, you'll be supporting the next frightened woman."

Dr. Orgel came in and gave Liza a hug. He whispered something in her ear, and she nodded and smiled. As Liza left, he turned to Dotty. "So far so good. How do you feel?"

"Not too bad."

"I want to see you in a week to do some blood work. We have to make sure the chemotherapy hasn't suppressed your bone marrow making your white cells, red cells, or platelets low. You need enough of those cells to prevent infection, anemia or bleeding. Remember we talked about that."

Dotty nodded. "I have a question. When will I lose my hair?"

"Maybe never, but the odds increase with each treatment."

"Can I color my hair in the meantime?"

"I'm afraid not. The definitive study hasn't been done, but there is some evidence that hair coloring might counteract the effects of the chemotherapy."

"You're lucky," I said. "Your hair will be getting lighter like mine." When Dr. Orgel left, I could see Dotty wasn't happy about not being able to color her hair. "Didn't your son buy you a Mickey Mouse baseball cap when he went to Disney World? Chuck says you look adorable, and I agree. To me, you're beautiful, with white hair, gray hair or no hair. Stop fixating on what you have no control over, and focus on how good our lives will be when this ordeal is over."

"I guess you're right, but . . ."

Before she could finish the sentence, I interrupted. "The fluids are finished. Let me get the nurse so we can go home."

When the nurse removed the IV, she told Dotty to continue the Zofran for another day, to ensure she wouldn't become nauseated or vomit. "See you next time," the nurse said. "Call if there are any problems."

On the way home in the car, I kept sneaking sideways glances at Dotty. I tried to assure myself that she was okay—that the chemotherapy didn't have any effect on her now and wouldn't in the future. Somehow, I couldn't get the image of Aaron out of my mind.

Chapter Nine

—Where's Doctor Z

The following week, we went to Dr. Orgel's office for the blood work. I hoped Dotty's clotting factors weren't low. I remembered the horrible death my mother suffered from bleeding into her brain. The fresh bruise on Dotty's thigh had stirred up this recollection. As they drew the blood, I tensed more than Dotty. Please God, let it be normal. The technician ran the blood through a machine that hummed before spitting out a colorful printout, replete with graphs, of her lab data. As we waited for Dr. Orgel to give us the results, my agitation became palpable to me and visible to Dotty.

"What's the matter?" she asked.

"Just tired."

"Yeah, sure."

"I guess I'm a little worried, but I'm sure everything will be fine."

"I hope so."

Dr. Orgel came into the lab, and after inquiring how Dotty was doing, looked at the printout. "Not bad," he said. "The white count and platelets are a little down, but not significantly. You should be all set to go for your second round of chemotherapy in two weeks. Any questions?"

Still thinking of my mother, I asked, "How low are the platelets?" I knew that anything below fifty thousand would put Dotty at increased risk of bleeding.

"One hundred and ten thousand."

"That's great." He handed me the results of her other studies and as he had said, they were a little lower than before, but no cause for concern.

On the way home, I explained the results to Dotty. She nodded. "Everything sounds good," she said.

I smiled. "Up for going out to lunch?"

"You bet."

Two weeks later we were sitting in the waiting room, hoping to be called back soon. The wait was interminably long. I put my arm around Dotty, as much to keep it from shaking, as to comfort her. Staring at all the women, with either shaved heads or fancy head coverings, had re-triggered my consternation.

"What's taking so long?" Dotty asked.

Liza, who was sitting next to us, answered. "Sometimes, the morning round of chemotherapy runs over. They have to clean the room and scrub it down. When that happens, it takes longer."

"We won't be done until late," Dotty said. "Maybe six-thirty, seven. I hope Dr. Orgel's still around when we're done."

"Don't you worry about that," Liza said. "He'll stay with us till the end, ay. Not like the jerk of an internist I had who hardly talked to me after I was diagnosed."

"What do you mean?"

"Wish I knew. This man had taken care of me for fifteen years. I thought we had become friends. When he gave me the results of the mammogram, he couldn't look me in the eye. He sent me off to the surgeon, then the oncologist, and that was the end of his involvement. There was no hug, no come in and see me anytime so we can talk, no how are you calls."

Dotty took Liza's hands into hers. "I can't understand a jerk like that."

Liza shrugged.

We continued sitting in silence waiting for the therapy to start. I thought about what Liza had said. I hadn't slept well the night before, and my eyes drifted shut. Soon, the movie in my mind started up.

As I entered her hospital room, Carrie's blue eyes darted to the door and fixed on my stethoscope adorned with clip-on animals and cartoon characters. "Where's Dr. Z?" she asked.

"I'm sure he'll be here tomorrow," I lied. "But he told me to give you this." I walked over to her bed, took the six-year-old in my arms and planted a kiss on her forehead. I pushed a lock of curly blond hair from in front of her eyes, and stared at her pale body studded with bruises. She buried her head in my shoulder and cried.

I looked at Joan Simpson, Carrie's mother, forcing myself to smile. "Dr. Z asked me to come by and examine this beautiful lady."

Joan knew who I was from the office so she just nodded. I sensed she wasn't happy about Dr. Z's absence.

I placed my stethoscope on Carrie's nose and rested my hand on her Walt Disney night shirt, lifting it slowly to examine her swollen abdomen.

"Mickey Duck is cute," I said.

"Mickey Mouse!"

"No, Donald Mouse and Mickey Duck."

She pushed the stethoscope off her nose and smiled. "You're weird," she said.

I brushed my hand on her stomach and pushed, noting an enlarged liver and spleen. Why didn't Dr. Z come see Carrie? He knew how sick she was—how much she would need him—how much she loved him. I found myself getting angry. Why did he leave me to talk to the parents? I hardly knew them.

I needed to collect myself. I gave Carrie a hug and told her mother I'd be right back to talk. I wanted to review Carrie's chart. I walked to the desk, took off my glasses, rubbed my eyes and flipped the pages of her chart. The fact that her blood smear was abnormal gave credence to my suspicion. Carrie had acute lymphocytic leukemia. It would take a hematology consult and a bone marrow exam to confirm my fear, but I was almost 100% sure.

I picked up the phone and called my partner, reviewing my findings with him. "I think she has leukemia. You need to get over and talk to the parents."

"I'm busy. I have an office full of patients and can't break away. Do me a favor and you tell them."

"Mel. They know and trust you. I've only met them a few times. Get your ass over here!"

"I'm asking you a favor. Please do it. I'll even work a night for you. I'm just too busy. I, I can't talk to them now." His voice continued to crack. "I'll, I'll talk to you later. Gotta run."

I sat at the nurses station and trembled. I thought back to my time as an air force pediatrician. We made the diagnosis of leukemia on a young child and I told the intern to speak to the parents.

He became ashen. "I can't do it," he said. "Please don't make me. I'll do anything you ask. I, I . . ." He stammered and his arms shook. I agreed to tell the parents if he would sit and observe. I remember thinking later that this was the best teaching I had ever done. Could my partner be like this intern and because of his own fears and insecurities be unable to handle these situations? He's a good pediatrician. How could this be?

As I reentered Carrie's room, I watched her shaking her index finger at a small blond doll. "You're a bad girl. I told you not to go out in the rain. Now you're sick. Bad girl."

"What's your dolly's name?" I asked.

"Sara. She's been very bad."

"Is it okay if I examine her?"

Carrie nodded.

I picked up the doll, placed my stethoscope on her chest, and looked in her ears with my otoscope. "Sara's going to be fine. She just has a little infection. Going out in the rain didn't make her sick. A lot of children and grownups go out in the rain without getting sick. A little rest and a lot of hugs and kisses from you will make her better.

Carrie smiled. She took Sara and squeezed. I gave Carrie a hug and signaled her mother to follow me outside. "We'll be right back, sweetheart," I said.

We walked into the waiting room. Carrie's father, David, was propped against the wall. He partly covered the frown on his face with his hand. I introduced myself, as I had never met him before.

"Where's Dr. Z?" he asked.

I explained that I was covering for him. I didn't know what else to say. I certainly couldn't promise that Dr Z would be there the next day. "Let's talk about Carrie's illness," I said. "How long has she been sick?"

Joan grabbed her husband's arm. "She's had a fever for about a month. We took her to see Dr. Z several times. He said it was a virus. Yesterday, he did a blood count and rushed us into the hospital for more tests."

Mel must have suspected. "I can understand why Dr Z thought Carrie had a viral illness. That's always a good possibility, but the tests we ran didn't show this."

"What's wrong, then?" Joan asked.

I swallowed hard before answering and shifted my weight from one foot to the other, like a prize fighter entering a fray he couldn't win. "She's a pretty sick little girl. Her . . ."

"Please, just tell me what's wrong with her," Joan said again.

"I can't be one hundred percent sure." I swallowed the spittle damming my throat. "But all the tests so far indicate that Carrie has leukemia. I'd like to have a pediatric oncologist see her."

Joan cried and buried her head in David's chest. He clung to her while she stammered. "How, how did this happen? What did we do wrong?"

"We really don't know what causes leukemia. It's just a freakish quirk, where the body breaks down and white cells divide out of control." I put my arm around Joan. "Going out in the rain didn't do this. Since we really don't know the reason the body does this, there's nothing you could have done that would have prevented her illness."

David looked up from comforting his wife, still stroking her head. "What's going to happen?" he asked.

"The good news is that leukemia is very treatable. It's not like the old days. Most children survive and do well."

"What kind of treatment? Not like those poisons that cause you to lose your hair and make you very sick?"

I nodded.

"Oh my poor little girl. My poor baby."

"We won't know which medicines in particular she'll need until the oncologist sees her," I said. "She'll need to do a bone marrow exam to find out what kind of leukemia Carrie has."

"That'll hurt, won't it?" Joan asked.

"Some, but we'll need to do it in order to find out what drugs to treat her with."

"There's more than one kind of leukemia?" Joan asked. "Does she have a kind that's easy to treat. Please God, make it so."

"We'll know more after the oncologist sees Carrie. I'm sure after I leave you'll have a thousand more questions and we'll be doing a lot more talking. We have an excellent pediatric oncologist here, who has taken care of hundreds of children with leukemia. Is it okay if I ask Dr. Springer to see Carrie? I'll be in a better position to answer your questions after she comes."

Joan and David nodded, and grasped each other. Joan sobbed. "Why God? Why our little girl?"

"You have to be strong for Carrie's sake," I said. "She's really going to need you. As frightened as you are, you can imagine how scared Carrie will be."

They nodded as they continued to cling to each other. I told them I was going to see Carrie and they should join me when they felt up to it. "Just give us a few minutes," Joan said.

As I entered Carrie's room, she was still sitting on her bed scolding her doll, then hugging it. "Do you like to play games?" I asked.

"Of course I do," she answered.

"Would you like to play tic-tac-toe?"

"That's a silly game. I used to play it with my daddy all the time, but it always ended in a tie. My daddy says there's no way to win that game."

"You don't know until you try."

I drew the nine-squared board and we placed our Xs and Os in the boxes. Carrie yelled. "I win."

"I want a rematch. Let's play again."

She nodded and the results were the same.

"You're too good for me," I said.

"You're letting me win."

"No I'm not. If you want something bad enough, you can win at anything." I said. "Take your sickness, for instance. You're going to have to take a lot of medicines and do a lot of things that aren't fun. I know you want to get better, and just like tic-tac-toe, if you try hard enough, before you know it, you'll be running around playing with your friends again."

Carrie threw her arms around me, as tears ran down her cheeks. I squeezed her back. "Everything will be okay."

We stayed this way for several minutes until the Simpsons returned. I excused myself. "I'll be back to see her tomorrow. In the meantime Dr. Springer will see her. If you have any questions, call me anytime." I scribbled my home phone number on back of my card and handed it to them.

David stared at the card. "Thank you. Do me a favor, please ask Dr. Z to stop by."

I nodded and left the room. I sensed Dr. Z would not be coming.

My eyes fluttered open when the nurse called us to start the chemotherapy. Dotty was pale. "I feel queasy," she said.

"Did you take the Zofran?"

She nodded.

"They'll give you more once the IV is started."

Dotty seemed more agitated than during the first round of chemotherapy. "What's the matter?" I asked.

"I was thinking about Liza's internist. What kind of doctor is that? What's become of medicine? It used to be different. Doctors cared. Now it's all about, show me the money. I hope that doesn't happen to me."

I didn't want to start a discussion and increase Dotty's anxiety. There might be other reasons for Liza's doctor's behavior, but I just nodded.

Dotty rested on the recliner and I held her hand. We were next to Liza again. I wondered if in her own worried state, Liza thought of how she could make things easier for Dotty. I had heard of the sisterhood of breast cancer survivors. Could this be an example? I hoped so. The nurse came over, jabbed Dotty's arm and administered the Zofran. We were off and running.

Dotty turned to Liza. "I'm sorry about what happened to you with your internist."

"Me too. But it taught me a lesson. Don't take anything or anyone for granted. Be on guard. Take responsibility for your own care."

That's a cynical attitude, I thought. You have to trust people—a doctor, a loved one, a friend.

Liza shifted position so that she faced Dotty. "At the time I was diagnosed, my husband and I were having troubles. Instead of drawing us closer, he up and left."

"A real shithead," Dotty said.

"Yeah!," Liza said. "You're lucky. You have someone who cares."

Dotty smiled and squeezed my hand. "Yes I am."

After listening to the women talk, I could see why Liza was so cynical. I excused myself to go to the bathroom. I did this as much to allow Dotty and Liza time to have woman talk, as a need to relieve myself. As I walked past several women who looked particularly ill, I wondered how anyone could abandon them—a physician, or especially a husband.

In the bathroom, I washed my face and stared in the mirror. Staring back at me was Mel. "I'm sorry," he mouthed.

*   *   *

I left Carrie's room and exited the hospital. Walking slowly toward my office where my car was parked. I was forced to quicken my pace when a light drizzle started. The ominous clouds suggested much worse. I felt sorry for Carrie and her family. I knew the ordeal that they faced would be so daunting, that it was almost beyond my comprehension. I was angry at Mel. How could he not come to see Carrie and her parents. Instead of getting into the car, I went into the office to talk to him.

I watched from the doorway of an examining room as he examined a little girl sitting on his lap. First he listened to the girl's chest, then the doll's. He repeated the procedure looking in both their ears. "You two are going to be fine," he said. "You just need to take a little of this medicine that I'm giving to your mom, and you need to eat this lollipop I found in your ear.

The little girl smiled and threw her arms around him. "I love you, Dr. Z."

As he walked into the hall, I jumped in front of him. "Mel, we have to talk."

"Can't it wait? I'm busy."

"No! We have to talk now."

I tugged on his sleeve and pulled him into my office. I pulled a lollipop out of his shirt pocket, and sucked on it to relieve my dry mouth. "Mel, how could you not come over? The Simpsons kept asking for you."

"I was busy. Besides, I'm no good in these situations."

"What do you mean, you're no good?"

Mel leaned back in his chair and rubbed his eyes. "Carrie is such a sweet little girl. I kind of suspected she had leukemia when I admitted her. I just don't want to see her so sick. I can't handle it."

"There you go again. What do you mean you can't handle it? You're a good doctor and a caring pediatrician. How can you back away from them just when they need you?"

He stammered. "What good would I be to them if I can't hold it together? I'd just screw up and make things worse."

"Why?"

"Long story. Please, you take care of her. Besides, you have more experience with leukemia than I do."

As he got up to leave the room, I shouted after him. "What you're doing is not fair to the Simpsons, and for that matter to me. So screw you."

On the way out, Kathy, Mel's daughter and nursing assistant, grabbed me. "I can understand why you'd be hurt, but did you ever stop and think what motivated his behavior?"

I shrugged. "No, but I'm sure you're going to tell me."

"Before you came to town my father was taking care of this cute five-year-old girl with acute lymphoma. She was a good friend of my sister's and was like another daughter to my dad.

When Jill died, my father went to pieces. For a while, he was no good to either his family or the practice. He had trouble handling it. With time, he was able to care for acutely ill kids, and as you know, he's quite good at it."

I nodded.

"But he hasn't been able to care for children with long term chronic illnesses, particularly those children with cancer. Talk things out with dad. Give him another chance."

"I'm sorry, I didn't know. But . . ." My anger hadn't abated. I turned to go home. "I'll think about what you said."

She shouted after me. "Good, that's all I ask."

I finished washing my face. When I got back to Dotty's side, the first drug was already dripping into her vein. "You okay?" I asked.

She nodded. "I feel better. Poor Liza doesn't look so good. She's not as upbeat as last time. I told her if she feels like talking, she should call me."

I smiled. "Good for you." Role reversal, I thought.

The nurse came and switched IV bags. As the second drug dripped into Dotty's vein, sweat broke out on her forehead. "I feel queasy," she said. "I'm hot all over."

"I'll get the nurse," I said.

Seconds later, the nurse and I returned. She took Dotty's blood pressure, and measured her heart and breathing rate. "Everything's good," the nurse said. "May be a very mild allergic reaction. No need to stop the therapy. Dr. Orgel likes to give IV benadryl in these situations. I'll just check with him."

"I hope Dr. Orgel comes," Dotty said. "I'm a little frightened."

It was as if he was listening to her. He came to her side, held her hand and examined her. "Nothing to worry about. It may be a mild allergic reaction, but I don't think so. It may be nerves. But to be sure, we'll give you some IV benadryl. It might make you a little sleepy, which is a good thing."

When the second drug was done, Dotty was feeling better. Liza had finished her therapy and was leaving. "I'll call you and we'll do lunch." Liza said.

Dotty nodded. "You bet."

When Liza left and the third drug was dripping into her vein, Dotty's eyes closed. The benadryl must have made her sleepy. I was glad Dotty had made a friend. Perhaps, they could help each other through the tribulations that lay ahead. Soon I joined Dotty in the arms of Morpheus. The image of Mel was soon before me.

It was several months later. I had procrastinated in speaking to Mel. I thought about what Kathy had said to me, but because of my anger, remained aloof toward my partner. Carrie had left the hospital and was in complete remission. She was coming to see me that afternoon. By, that time, we had established a close bond.

I sat at my desk eating a tongue sandwich. Maybe it wasn't all Mel's fault. I understood why he behaved that way, although I couldn't condone his behavior. Perhaps my motives weren't so pure. I enjoyed a challenge and thrived on seeing a critically ill child recover. Somehow, I was guarded against the lows, and satisfied with the knowledge that I had done my best—content that I could help families regardless of the outcome. I thought about Aaron. I realized that Mel needed his world to be on an even keel, free of the roller coaster ride that caring for a chronically ill patient would provide. His past experiences had ingrained that in him. We all had our strong points. His was caring for acutely ill patients who would soon be better. Mine was the long term care of families, forging lasting bonds with them, so that I could help them through life's lows, and share with them life's highs. But at least Mel could have given me a heads up and not let me march blindly into a situation, like I had done with Carrie Simpson.

I stuck my head into Mel's office. He was leafing through a journal. "Kathy explained to me why you shy away from potentially terminally ill patients. But you can't dump these patients on me without so much as a word."

"Look, I know you're pissed, but believe me it was for the best. Carrie is in good hands. I'll make it up to you. I really will."

"Promise me though, if this ever happens again, you'll at least warn me. I don't want to go into this kind of situation blind again."

"You've got it. I'll try not to dump a patient like Carrie on you again, but I probably won't succeed. I will clue you in, though. It really was wrong of me to leave you out to dry like that. No hard feelings?"

I shrugged and walked away. I was still angry at the way he had treated me, but at least I understood some of his reasons, and was pleased by the sincerity of his apology.

That afternoon, Carrie came to the office for a checkup. She raced down the hall and flew into my arms. I twirled her, which was becoming more difficult for me, as she had gained back the weight she had lost during the acute phase of her illness, and then some. As Joan Simpson followed her down the hall, Dr Z was standing there. "Hi Joan," he said. "It's really good to see you. Dr. W tells me how great Carrie's doing. I'm so glad."

Joan plowed right past him without as much as an acknowledgment. I watched as his shoulders sagged and his chin drooped. He stood there, fixed in the hallway, until two boys ran up to him and grabbed his hands. "Come on Dr. Z, let's finish our game." Mel squeezed their hands, lifted his head and smiled, before picking each one up under an arm and walking them into his office.

All afternoon I thought about how good Mel was with patients—how much I missed our friendly rivalry on the basketball and tennis courts. I saw him sitting at his desk typing up a chart, so I stuck my head through the door. "How'd you like to go for a beer after work," I said.

"I'd like that."

"Me too."

I was awakened from the movie in my mind by Dotty's urgent voice. "Paul, the IV's finished. Get the nurse. Let's go home."

I rubbed my eyes. "Yeah, sure."

As we were leaving, Dotty leaned on me. "Still a little shaky," she said. "But I'm glad it's over. Two down, four to go. I hope it doesn't keep getting worse with each session."

"I don't think so."

"Does Dr. Orgel want me to come back for blood work before the next round?"

"In ten days, he said."

As we got into the car, Dotty plunked herself into the front seat and struggled with the belt buckle."

"Let me help."

"No, I can do it myself."

"I know you can."

Dotty wiped her eyes. "I'm sorry I yelled." After a few seconds, she clicked the belt and stared at me. "I hope Liza calls."

I reached across the seat and squeezed Dotty's hand. "Me too. If not, call her."

Dotty nodded.

Chapter Ten

–Tureen

The night before Dotty was to have her blood work, I lay in bed staring at her sleeping on her back. I shivered, thinking my mother looked that way the last time I saw her—after she bled into her brain and lapsed into a coma. I feared Dotty's platelet count would be suppressed by the chemotherapy, subjecting her to a similar fate. I felt guilty over my perceived blame for my mother's death. I had to get these thoughts out of my mind or I'd be no use to Dotty. I had to focus on better times. I closed my eyes, hoping for a respite from my anxiety—hoping the movie in my mind would play happy times with my mother.

"Paul, the principal wants to see you."

I stood shaking, as my eighth grade teacher, Mrs. Goldfarb, spoke to me. "Why? What did I do?"

She shrugged. "I don't know. The note the monitor just brought in says you're to go to his office, now."

As I left the classroom and walked through the halls, I trembled and wondered why I had been summoned. When I entered the principal's office, his secretary told me to have a seat—he'd be with me in a minute. I stared at a portrait of a man named John Dewey and wondered who he was. The only Dewey I knew was Thomas Dewey who had lost the presidency to Harry Truman a few years before. My brother had pleaded with my parents not to put in a protest vote for Henry Wallace—that Truman had a chance to win.

Fortunately, even though these protest votes cost Truman New York State, he was able to eke out a victory.

I tried to think of some reason that I was here. Had someone reported me for pulling Rosalie Lasnock's hair again? Was it because I was late for home room the last few days, lingering in the school yard to finish a game of hoops? My school work was okay. I hadn't failed anything.

Before I came to any conclusion, the principal called me into his office. He was a tall man with slicked back black hair, and a paunch protruding over the pants of his double breasted, blue pinstriped suit.

"Why am I here?" I asked Mr. Aronoff. "I didn't do anything wrong, did I?"

He shook his head. "You missed the exam for Stuyvesant yesterday."

"Nobody ever told me about it."

"It was a mis-communication. They called this morning and said you can take the tenth grade exam being given this afternoon. But even if you pass, you'll still have to start in ninth grade."

"That's not fair," I said. "There will be a lot of stuff on the exam, like algebra, that I haven't had yet."

"All you can do is your best. I called your mother and she's driving to school to pick you up and take you to Stuyvesant, so that you can get there in time for the exam."

"But my mother doesn't know how to drive."

Mr. Aronoff shrugged. "That's what she said. Maybe your mother is coming with a neighbor or something. She asked that you wait for her by the front entrance to the school. Here's a pass allowing you to leave the building and excusing you for the rest of the day."

Taking the slip of paper from Mr. Aronoff, I walked slowly, looking at my saddle shoes. I was worried about passing the advanced tenth grade test. I wondered what my mother was up to and how she could pick me up in a car?

As I stood by the entrance to the school, a yellow Checker Cab screeched to a stop. My mother stuck her head out the window. "Come, Bubbeleh. You're going to be late for the exam."

Getting into the cab, I hugged my mother. "We can't afford this," I said. "Can we?"

"When it comes to you and your education, money is no object."

As the cab roared up Flatbush Avenue, past the large arch at the Grand Army Plaza, I said, "I'm a little worried about the exam. Do you know I have to take the tenth grade test?"

My mother nodded. "You'll do the best you can. If you don't get into Stuyvesant it won't be the end of the world. Erasmus is a good school."

"But Mickey said Stuyvesant is one of the best schools in the city. Dad agrees"

"I'm sure you'll do well anywhere you go. Besides, I have a feeling you're going to pass the test for Stuyvesant."

"I'm glad one of us thinks so."

My mother reached out and hugged me. I squeezed back. "I love you," she said.

"I love you, too, Ma."

The cab dropped us off at Union Square, several blocks from Stuyvesant. "I'm going to shop at Kleins," my mother said. She pointed to the front entrance. "I'll meet you over there when you're finished." Mom kissed me good-bye and wished me luck. I trudged the four blocks to Stuyvesant, arriving with ten minutes to spare. As I sat at a desk waiting for the proctor to give out the exam, I looked at all the other boys sitting there for the same purpose. *Maybe it won't be so bad if I don't pass. Then, at least, I'll be able to go to school with girls.*

I opened up the test booklet and stared at the first question. *Reduce X squared + 4X +4 = 0 to its lowest terms and solve for X.* What the hell did that mean? Fortunately, it was multiple choice and I tried to work backwards. The choices were, 2, -2, 4, and -4. Maybe I should solve the problem like a square root? The square root of nine is 3, (3x3). Reducing X squared + 4X + 4 = 0 the same way, I came up with X+2 times X+2. X had to be 2 or could it be -2. If I put X+2 = 0 then, when you moved +2 to the other side of the equation it would have to be -2, wouldn't it? I wasn't sure, but it seemed logical so I bubbled in -2 as the answer.

I wiped my forehead and continued through the math portion of the exam in this vein. The English portion wasn't any easier. There were a lot of words whose meaning I didn't know and was forced to guess at the answers. The exam ended three hours later and I was sure that I wouldn't be going to Stuyvesant. It just wasn't fair that I had to take the tenth grade exam.

By the time I left the school, it was getting dark. I walked through a chilly drizzle to meet my mother at Kleins. Stopping to buy a soft pretzel from a peddler's cart, I munched as I wended my way. When my mother saw me, she raced forward carrying a full shopping bag in one hand and an open umbrella in the other. "Come under the umbrella," she yelled. "You're drenched."

We entered Kleins to seek refuge from the rain. After wiping me with a handkerchief, she asked, "So, how did you do?"

I shook my head and scrunched my lips. "It was all stuff I didn't know."

"I'm sure you did fine," she said. "I was in the Sporting Goods Department and picked out a present for you. I wanted you to see it before I bought it."

"What?"

"Come, you'll see."

When we got to the Sporting Goods Department, my mother walked up to a particular salesman who brought out a box from under the counter. "Do you like it?" my mother asked.

"Are you kidding. I've always wanted an official NBA basketball." I reached up and kissed my mother. "I love it. Thank you."

As we left the store, she asked, "How would you like to go to dinner at Schrafts?"

"You bet I would. Schrafts has the best ice cream in the world."

At Schrafts, I ate a double cheeseburger with fries and for dessert had my favorite, a vanilla sundae with butterscotch syrup and crushed nuts, topped with a cherry.

"How are the Dodgers doing?" my mother asked.

"Ma, you know it's winter and they're not playing. Last year, they blew a big lead to the Giants and lost the pennant in a playoff game when Bobby Thomson hit a home run in the ninth inning."

"That's right. You told me. I'm sure they'll do better this year."

I smiled. "I hope so."

When we left, the rain had stopped, and we walked towards the subway. In one arm I clutched the basketball. The other arm was locked around my mother's wide waist. She stroked the top of my head, which drooped onto her shoulder. "You look tired, Bubbeleh. Why don't we take a cab home?"

"Really?" I asked.

She smiled. "Really!"

Several weeks later, when I came home from school, my mother was in the kitchen. She had on a gravy stained apron, and was cooking my favorite dish, macaroni and cheese with crushed carrots.

"There's a letter for you on the breakfast room table," she said.

I picked up the letter, trembling as I read. *"Congratulations, you have been accepted to Stuyvesant High School. We hope . . .*

I ran to my mother, and threw my arms around her. Handing her the letter, I smiled.

"I knew you could do it," she said.

I untied her apron, which fell to the floor. "You rascal," she said. She feigned anger and chased me down the hall. I stopped and flung myself at her, grabbing her around the waist. I squeezed hard as she stroked the top of my head. After a few minutes, she started to back away, but I refused to let go. I clutched tighter trying hard not to lose hold of her.

The next day, on the way to have Dotty's blood tested, I thought about my mother taking me to my high school entrance exam, about our fun trip to Canada, and about her premature death from a brain bleed. I had to get the latter out of my mind, or Dotty would pick up on my angst and transfer it to herself. She had enough of her own and didn't need mine.

We waited to have the blood work done until Dr. Orgel's technician returned from lunch. Liza was also waiting and Dotty immediately struck up a conversation. "You look a little pale, Liza. Are you okay?"

"Yeah, sure. Just a little tired. Thanks for asking. How are you doing?"

"Okay, I guess, but still scared out of my mind. My son's going to take us to Disney World, after the next round of chemo, to get my mind off this business." Dotty waved her hand around the room. "I hope nothing interferes with that."

"You're lucky to have such a great support system." Liza looked at me. "Your husband, your children. I've got no one."

Dotty put her arm around Liza. This is a definite role reversal, I thought. Maybe it would do them both good. With all the thoughts about my mother, I didn't think I was a great support system.

When we were called into the lab, Dotty stuck out her left arm to have the blood drawn. "I need the other arm," the technician said. "We can't use the same side as the mastectomy and node dissection."

"I know that," Dotty said. "I just forgot."

As the blood was being analyzed, thoughts of my mother's death flooded my mind. I watched the machine spit out the results and tried to sneak a peek, but had no luck. We would have to get them from Dr. Orgel. When he came in and looked at the printout, I tried to read his face, without success. "Everything's good." he said.

What's the platelet count?" I asked.

"Ninety-four thousand. No risk of bleeding, and the hemoglobin and white count are slightly low, but not dangerous."

He handed me the piece of paper, and I studied it before smiling. "I guess we're good for the next round of chemotherapy?"

"You bet," Dr Orgel said. "Everything's a go. See you next week."

I put my hand up to high five Dotty, but she just smiled and winked. "I don't know why everyone is so happy that I can have more of that sickening junk injected into my veins."

On the way home, Dotty didn't talk much, and what she had to say had little to do with her. "I'm worried about Liza," she said.

"I know, and I'm sure you'll do all you can. But you've got to take care of yourself."

Dotty didn't say anything, but I sensed she was unhappy with my response, as she didn't say anything else the rest of the way. Maybe she wanted me to make more of an effort to comfort Liza. I was having a difficult enough time comforting Dotty given my own nervous state, no less helping someone else.

When we got home, Dotty excused herself. "I need to take a nap."

I sat in my father's recliner and stared at the picture of my mother and father on the table. I closed my eyes trying to think of simpler times from my childhood. Images of our trip to Canada crystalized.

In her kitchen, my mother was trying to emulate my grandmother's chopped liver by churning a hand-held grinder, and watching the chicken liver, fried onions, schmaltz and hard boiled eggs ooze through the pores. I snuck up and threw my arms around the plastic apron covering her ample girth, reacting with exuberance to her news. "Bubbeleh, we're all going to your brother's graduation."

My parents and uncle and aunt would drive to Chicago. I would take the overnight Twentieth Century Limited to Chicago where I would meet them for the final leg of our journey, so that we could all be with my brother when he received his Masters Degree from The University of Illinois. I had to finish several high school regents examinations first. Knowing my father's driving ability, I hoped we'd get there safely. My mother told me that after the graduation the six of us would take a week-long automobile trip through Canada and Niagara Falls. I kissed my mother, grabbed her pudgy hands and we began to dance across the yellow linoleum floor with the grace of two smiling water buffaloes.

Several weeks later, I traipsed through Grand Central Station observing in awe the seething mass of humanity as they scurried to the train platforms. I stepped onto the maroon carpet leading to the Twentieth Century Limited. I was fifteen, traveling on my own for the first time. I was excited about my adventure, but filled with anxiety.

In 1953 the Twentieth Century Limited was a relatively expensive way to travel. It was an all Pullman, no coach train, which made the trip from New York to Chicago in sixteen hours, leaving late in the afternoon and arriving early the next morning. I was pleased my parents had spent the extra fare for me to travel on the Limited. We couldn't afford for me to eat meals in the elegant dining car, so I came well fortified with provisions.

As the porter showed me to my Pullman room, I passed through the club car, noting portly men dressed in suits, sitting in plush red leather chairs, smoking cigars and sipping brandy. I imagined that this was like spending an afternoon in one of the downtown gentlemen's clubs. Even then, I thought how decadent they were, wasting money on frivolity. I must admit, though, I was glad to be in a Pullman, no matter how tiny my cubicle. I was too excited to sleep and sat on the bed munching Hershey bars and Good and Plenty candy. I listened to the grinding noise the wheels made on the tracks and looked at the brightly-lit countryside. I was thinking ahead to our trip to Canada, an adventure I eagerly awaited.

The next morning the train pulled into the LaSalle Station in Chicago, where my parents waited for me. After a perfunctory hug and kiss, they whisked me into the car for a breakneck trip to reach my brother's graduation on time. I remember thinking, please God, let my father drive with some semblance of sanity. I want to complete this trip with all my body parts intact.

As we wove down the interstate traveling twenty five miles an hour above the speed limit, we were stopped by the flashing lights and siren of a trailing police car. My father stuck his head out the window and said, "I don't have time for this foolishness. My son is graduating from the University of Illinois." Fortunately, we were stopped by a dyed-in-the-wool Illini fan, who was not aggravated by my father's aggressive attitude. He let us go with a stern warning.

We arrived in time for the graduation. How proud I was watching my brother march across the stage in his cap and gown. I watched the fuss my family made and thought, someday I'd have an even more advanced degree and they would make a bigger fuss over me.

After we crammed my brother's luggage into the car, there was almost no room for people. The trunk was overloaded and would not close, having to be lashed down with rope. The luggage rack on top was piled high with suitcases. The inside of the car had bags and packages stuffed into every nook and cranny, including the back ledge. As I took my place in the middle of the back seat, I squished several plums. I looked somewhat sheepish, but when everyone laughed, I joined the merriment.

My recollections of the next week are somewhat hazy. What is vivid is my memory of this being a happy trip, filled with laughter. I remember my father running out of gas and having to walk several miles to a gas station, which we had passed earlier. "We've got plenty of gas to last us until we pull in for the night," he said. I remember my aunt asking a gas station attendant, "When do they turn off the falls?" She meant, when do they turn off the lights illuminating the falls at night. Her comment caused me to chortle and tease her, "They turn the falls off when it gets dark. They don't want anyone wading in and hurting themselves."

This exchange with my aunt led me to dub her sayings *Evelynisms,* named after her. Through the years there were many, but the second also occurred on this trip. She was talking about her best friend's son, president of the National Honor Society and how she had plotted to have her youngest daughter meet him. But my sixteen year old cousin, Sheila, was having nothing to do with my aunt's match-making machinations. My aunt told us that she finally said to Sheila, "What's the big deal? Why don't you just go out and make him?"

"Aunt Evelyn," I said. "You want your daughter to sleep with him even before she gets to know him. What kind of mother are you, anyway?"

My aunt's face turned from a peaches and cream complexion to a deep crimson. "I didn't mean that," she said. "All I wanted Sheila to do was to make his acquaintance."

I smiled and said, "Sure you didn't mean that."

I also remember the lush foliage I saw on the trip, the vast array of multicolor petunias and pansies and the graceful deer at a national park where we stopped by a meandering stream for a picnic lunch. I see images of the tree-lined streets and weathered parliament buildings in Ottawa and a staid church on top of Mount Royal. I recall feeling the stinging spray on my face while on the Maid of the Mist ferry in the thundering waters under Horseshoe Falls. I couldn't believe someone was crazy enough to go over the falls in a barrel.

* * *

I awoke in the chair with my arms wrapped around me. I was glad my thoughts were of happier moments, not of my mother's death. Maybe it would help me focus on supporting Dotty.

Dotty wasn't looking forward to the third round of chemotherapy, but luckily her fear was unwarranted, because it went smoothly. She wasn't burdened with the nausea, bothered by the sickly antiseptic smells, or by the wait. She was upset looking at and talking to Liza. When the IV was running and the first drug dripped into her vein, Dotty turned to me, and beckoned me to come closer, so that she couldn't be overheard by Liza who was behind the next curtain. Dotty cocked her head in that direction. "I really don't like the way Liza looks. She's pale, has lost all her hair, and is having trouble keeping up a conversation in the waiting room. I hope Dr. Orgel sees her before they give her the chemo."

I nodded. After a few minutes, we heard Liza talking to Dr. Orgel. He was trying to be upbeat, but the gravelly tone of his voice belied the fact. "Liza, you're running a fever, so we ran a blood count. The white cells and platelets are very low, increasing your risk for a blood stream infection or for serious bleeding. Remember, we talked about that?"

There was a pause, then Liza mumbled something that we couldn't hear.

"I know," Dr. Orgel said. "But we can't give you the therapy today. It would be dangerous. In fact, I'd like to admit you to the hospital, take blood cultures, and start you on high doses of antibiotics as a precaution."

Dotty's face reddened. "Poor Liza," she said. "I hope she's all right."

We listened as the nurse came and helped Liza into a wheelchair. When she was wheeled by our room, Dotty sat up. "Good luck. I'll call you."

Later, Dotty kept babbling. She confessed that when she looked at Liza, she saw herself. This was a feeling I too had been harboring. "There but for the grace of God go I," Dotty said.

"The situations different," I said. "You're doing great. In fact, you haven't lost a hair."

"I know, but Liza was to have finished her chemo today, and I still have three more sessions after this. I'm worried about her, and at the same time scared that it will happen to me."

"Even if she has a blood stream infection, it's treatable. It's a rare complication and unlikely to happen to you." I wished that I felt the confidence of my words. I bent over and kissed her forehead. "Why don't you close your eyes and rest?"

Dotty shrugged. "I'll try."

When she had drifted off, I felt relieved. At least for now, I wouldn't have to stifle my emotions, and keep up the transparency of an upbeat attitude. I was scared out of my wits, but didn't want to transmit those feelings to Dotty. I closed my eyes, trying to relax. Soon, I was back in Canada on our family trip.

What remain most clear in my mind are the stops at every antique barn along the way and the purchases we made. The first one we stopped at was a large red structure with many aisles laden with merchandise arranged in a haphazard manner. My mother sniffed her way up and down the aisles before smelling out a sterling silver coffee service, tucked between an ornate candelabra and a collection of old English fire irons. "We have to have this," My mother said. "I need a set like this to serve from at the Hadassah meetings at our house. I'm going to be president of the Brooklyn region next year."

The service consisted of five pieces, including an ornately carved tray. In the center of the tray was the large coffee urn with intricately grooved lines, forming a pattern bearing no resemblance to anything I had ever seen. The bottom of the urn stood on three funny looking carved feet. A spigot when pulled to the right would release coffee out of a spout at the bottom of the server. The smaller tea server had the same unappealing pattern and silly looking feet. The creamer and sugar holder mimicked the two larger pieces. I recall thinking, how could she like this. It's ugly.

My brother said, "I really like this, Mom. Why don't you get it."

My father chimed in, "I like it too, but we don't have any room in the car."

"Why not ship it, Pop?" my brother asked.

"That's a good idea," my father answered.

I remember thinking that if my brother likes it so much, why doesn't he offer to carry it on his lap. I excused myself to go to the bathroom and by the time I returned the package had been wrapped, paid for and arrangements made for shipping.

At another large barn filled with either junk or antiques depending on your point of view, my mother waded through the aisles, and like a bloodhound stalking its prey, sniffed out a soup tureen. "This is beautiful," she said. "But, we can't seem too eager. I'll bargain with the owner."

The large covered soup tureen, as well as the 15 inch round plate on which it sat, was rimmed by gold leaf, and was decorated with an ornate nineteenth century English scene. In the background was a castle reflected in a lake, framed by two spreading trees that were in full green foliage. In the foreground, a family leaned on a balustrade looking at the castle. They were dressed in the garb of the times, top hat and morning coat for the man, long dress and bonnet for the wife and matching attire for the children. Sprays of red and peach roses circled both pieces. Two fish on each side stuck out in opposite directions, their entwined tails forming handles for the tureen.

The lid again depicted the same scene and had two vertical fish with their tails enmeshed, forming a handle. Gold leaf framed the edges of the cover, and the colors, mostly greens, reds and tans, mirrored the tureen and plate.

The bottom of the plate had the word England imprinted on top of an octagon that contained the words, "1760/ Leeds/1878." Below the octagon, in black, was the phrase "Reproduced by Masons 1932," and underneath that in red letters, "L 75/W." The underside of the tureen had the same logo except the hand painted red letters were, "L 75/CK." My mother said the dating and numbering made the tureen quite valuable.

My father agreed that the tureen was beautiful and to my surprise, he even said it wasn't too expensive. However, he added, "We don't have one scintilla of room in the car to put such a big piece. It's too fragile to ship. We can't buy it."

My mother frowned and her eyes misted. "But it will look so perfect on the dining room table."

I didn't want to see my mother disappointed. Besides, I loved the tureen too. Even then, I was intrigued by the design, the clarity of its muted colors and its enormous size. My mouth watered thinking about the homemade vegetable and chicken soups I would be served from the tureen. "If we buy it, Pop, I'd be willing to hold it on my lap till we arrive home. Mom really loves the tureen."

Seeing my resolve, my father relented and told my mother to go bargain with the owner. My father would not be put out. It didn't matter how stuffed the car was, his seat would be unencumbered, as he was doing the bulk of the driving.

My mother scrambled to the front of the barn to agree on a price with the owner, before my father changed his mind. I was quite used to this negotiating process and always found it amusing. I remember my grandmother at similar bargaining sessions. Each time there was an offer she would say in Yiddish, "Come children, we go," until she received an irresistible offer she couldn't refuse.

My mother made an offer which the owner rejected and she turned to leave. The owner chased us into the parking lot and under the sign, "Big Ben's Discount Antiques," made a counter proposal. My mother shook her head, opened the car door and sat, rejecting his next offer too. The owner finally said, "Okay lady, I'll let you have it for twenty dollars more than your original offer." My mother smiled. The proprietor, Big Ben, boxed the tureen and I took my seat in the back holding it on my lap. I remember clutching the box the entire trip, as if by releasing my grip I would lose my hold on my mother.

"Paul, Paul," Dotty yelled. "You're clutching your chest. Are you okay?"

"Just a little cold."

"I'm the one that gets cold in the air conditioning, not you."

I shrugged. "How are you feeling?"

"A little nervous after what happened to Liza."

"I'm sure it's a temporary setback. She'll be okay, I think."

Dotty nodded. "I guess I know that. But . . ."

Before Dotty finished the sentence, the nurse came and started the last drug. When she left, Dotty wiped her eyes and cleared her throat. "I hope Liza is okay. I hope my blood work will be okay, so that we can go to Disney World with Chuck and Maureen in two weeks. They really wants to take us. See, I still have hopes."

I walked over to Dotty, grasped her unencumbered hand and squeezed. "I know, sweetheart. So do I."

Chapter Eleven

—Disney

The day before our weekend at Disney World, Dotty went in for blood work. She was looking forward to the trip, so I hoped her blood parameters hadn't reached dangerously low levels that would prevent us from going. Liza was still in the hospital fighting off the ravages of a bloodstream infection. Dotty visited her several times and said she looked awful. "She's still running a fever and is very weak, "Dotty said. "They obviously haven't gotten the infection under control."

I nodded. "Probably true, but I'm sure they'll find the right combination of antibiotics. They might have to remove her port. It sometimes serves as a source of infection. I'm sure glad you have good veins and didn't need one."

"Me too."

When we arrived at Dr. Orgel's office, the technician was waiting for us. We were ushered right back to the lab. I again watched Dotty's blood being sucked into the counting chamber of this impersonal, large black machine that reminded me of the proverbial black hole. I listened to the ensuing clicks emanating from the beast and waited for it to spit out the results. No longer did a person have to count the cells under a microscope like I did when I was a lab technician at Lenox Hill Hospital in New York, during my senior year in medical school.

Dr. Orgel came in and looked at the paper. "You're good to go," he said. "A little lower, but not bad."

"How low is not bad?" I asked. "What's the platelet count?"

"Eighty-four thousand."

I nodded. "Low, but not fifty thousand, the magic number that would have put Dotty at greatly increased risk of bleeding—bleeding into the brain like my mother."

On the way home, I snuck a peek at Dotty's hair that was turning gray, as she wasn't allowed to dye it. At least she hadn't lost any hair. I knew she felt the gray hair made her look old, and I had to try and dispel that notion,

"I see you looking at me," Dotty said.

"I can't help it. You're beautiful."

She ran her fingers through her hair. "Yeah, sure. Just keep your eyes on the road.

I smiled.

When we got home, we packed for the weekend and went out for a bite of dinner. When we got back, there was a message on the answering machine from Chuck, hoping all was well, and he'd pick us up at 10:00.

"We're going to have a ball," I said.

"I hope so."

Dotty turned in early and I went to the family room to watch test patterns on television. I was glad Dotty's platelets weren't too low, and she wasn't in any real danger of serious bleeding. Somehow, I just couldn't get the images of my mother out of my mind. I closed my eyes and was transported back to when I was sixteen years old, standing in front of the mirror in my room on Montgomery Street.

* * *

My last recollection of my mother was an argument we had the evening before her stroke. I had tried on a brown herringbone suit that my mother had bought for me. I looked in the mirror and hated the suit. I thought it was ugly and made me look even fatter than I was. I resented my mother for having purchased it without my being present.

My mother shouted through the closed door. "Come on out, Bubbeleh. Let's see how you look."

I eased the door open and walked into the dinette. "It's perfect," my mother said. "It looks so nice on you."

"No it doesn't. It's ugly! I hate it and I hate you for buying it for me. I wouldn't wear it to a dog fight."

I slammed the door to my room, ripped off the suit, and lay down on my bed and cried. The next morning my mother was taken to the hospital in a coma. She had a stroke with bleeding into her brain. Please God, let her recover. I need to apologize. How could those vile words be the last words my mother heard from me? Despite my prayers, she died several weeks later without ever regaining consciousness. Brain surgery proved as futile as my prayers. Why had God taken my mother at such an early age? It must have been to punish me for what I had done. I promised God that if I could only have her back, I'd become a doctor as she had wanted me to. Also, since she had worked so hard in Hadassah for the establishment of the state of Israel, I vowed someday I would fulfill her dream and stand in Israel in her place.

I was sixteen years old when my mother passed away in May of 1954. She was just 49 and had suffered a fatal stroke. I was assured it was due to a congenital condition; a weakness in the wall of a blood vessel that had given way and burst. I, on the other hand, was convinced that I had caused her death. I was devastated.

We followed the hearse that took her body to the cemetery. The feeling of guilt encompassed me like the dark clouds on this rainy day. Rain pelted the windows, further dampening my mood.

The cemetery was packed with weeping family and friends standing under umbrellas. My grandfather was stoical, although several tears clouded his eyes. My grandmother beat her breasts and glowered at my father. The look told me that she blamed him for my mother's death. My mother and father had been arguing about money for several years, and my grandmother had sided with her daughter. I couldn't understand why there had to be blame? Why did I have to blame myself? Why did my grandmother have to blame my father—and who knows whom my aunts and uncles blamed? But my feelings persisted.

After the service, we went back to my house to sit Shiva. The mirrors were draped in black, so that we wouldn't show vanity by looking in them. We sat on hard stools. We shouldn't be comfortable in our time of grief—we should suffer.

The dining room table was laden with food. There were platters of Nova Scotia salmon, bagels, cream cheese, and pounds of delicatessen meat. Cakes and cookies rimmed the food platters. Friends and family who would pay their respects needed to be well fed, as did we. It seemed ironic to me that we needed all this food so that we could gain strength to suffer.

People piled into our house. My family wasn't there. A close friend told us that my grandmother had decreed that henceforth no one would go into our house since she blamed my father for my mother's death. Unfortunately, when my grandmother spoke, all her adult children listened. What about me? Had she forgotten I lived there too? I went into my room, slammed the door, and ate a Baby Ruth bar stashed in my desk.

The next afternoon my brother, father and I were alone, sitting on stools, eating tongue sandwiches, telling endearing stories about my mother, when the doorbell rang. It was my grandfather. He trudged up the flight of stairs, breathing rapidly from the long walk from his house and the climb to our home on the second floor. He didn't have to tell me that he had defied my grandmother. I knew. I was surprised it was my grandfather who broke my grandmother's edict, since in all these years he had never honored his promise to do something with just me.

For the next year, until I went off to college, my grandfather came frequently. Mainly he was there on Friday nights after he finished at the tailor shop. He was exhausted from his arduous work and long walk. He brought a challah, said a motzi, and we had a Sabbath dinner that I bought at the store. I saw no other family member, in my house, again. I was grateful at least to have my grandfather at a time when my adolescent emotions were trying to cope with the death of my mother and my guilt in causing her demise.

I was startled by the thunderous applause on the TV. Some clown had jumped his motorcycle over a number of trucks and survived. I rubbed my eyes, and as I got ready for bed, I thought, please God, don't let what happened to my mother happen to Dotty. I hoped this prayer would be heard, not like the one I made when I was sixteen.

The next day, Chuck drove to Disney World, seating his mother next to him in the front. His wife, Maureen, and I sat in the back. We watched familiar scenery, citrus groves and freshly planted Sabal palm trees, while we reminisced about past trips to Disney World. "Dad, I hope you're not going to insist on going for ride after ride on It's a Small World, like the old days," Chuck said.

"Why? It's a great way to see the sites through the eyes of cute, singing costumed dolls." I looked at Dotty and smiled. "You'd like me to take you around the world, wouldn't you?"

She rolled her eyes and returned my smile.

Chuck shook his head, but I noticed a broad grin on his face.

When we reached the hotel, we unpacked and went to the Magic Kingdom. Dotty put on the Mickey Mouse baseball cap that Chuck had bought for her. She was self conscious about being in public with whitening hair. "You look adorable, mom," Chuck said.

"You think so?"

We all nodded.

After a few minutes of walking, Dotty was exhausted. We sat down on a bench to rest. "Wait here," Chuck said. He returned in a few minutes pushing a wheel chair he had rented. "Hop aboard, mom." Chuck pushed Dotty around the rest of the weekend. The added bonus was that since Dotty was in a wheel chair, we went to the front of all the lines.

"I promise," I said. "I'll only go on It's a Small World once." I took Dotty's hand and we ambled down the ramp, followed by Chuck and Maureen.

"Brings back old times," I said.

Dotty nodded. "Yeah, good times."

"They'll be good again."

We spent the day going from ride to ride and ate dinner at Cinderella's Castle. When we got back to the hotel, Dotty was dragging.

"We're going to a new club in one of the parks," Chuck said. "Why don't you guys join us?"

Dotty shook her head. "Thanks, but I'm too tired. You go and have fun."

"I think I'll stay with mom. Have a good time."

When they left, I held Dotty's hand. "Oh to be young."

She smiled. I'm having a good time, but I can't stop worrying about Liza."

"She'll be okay. You deserve a little respite."

"I guess you're right."

We got ready for bed and fell asleep in each other's arms.

The next day we went to the new theme park, Animal Kingdom. Because Dotty was in a wheel chair, we boarded the safari train without waiting. We watched animals frolicking in their natural environment. I wondered if there was any frolicking left for Dotty and me.

As we exited the park, a young boy broke free of his mother's grasp, and ran down the path. When she called him, he turned his head, tripped over a bench, and smashed his forehead into the concrete walkway, opening a large gash. As I was closest to him, I pulled out a handkerchief and applied pressure to the cut. The boy wasn't unconscious and was crying, both good signs that there was no bleeding into the brain. I called out for someone to call the paramedics. When they arrived, I left the lad in their hands. The mother thanked me as they whisked the boy to the first aid station.

"That was nice of you," Dotty said. "You've got blood on your shirt."

"All in a days work. I'll change when we get back to the room. That little fella is going to need a bunch of stitches to close that cut."

I looked at Dotty and visualized a gash on her forehead. With her low platelets it would be impossible to stop the bleeding. In all likelihood, from a fall like that, she would have bled into her brain. I had to get those thoughts out of my mind, but I kept visualizing my mother after she had her intra-cranial bleed, and lay comatose in her hospital room, before dying.

I was so distraught after her death that I was unable to concentrate. I even failed an academic subject, French. It was the only time this ever happened to me. My father and older brother decided it would be good for me to get out of the city for the summer. They found a job for me as a waiter in a summer camp in Connecticut. They were convinced the fresh air and hard work would take my mind off my mother.

I wanted to stay home. I didn't feel like doing anything. I fought with my father about this, but ultimately was forced to give in. "It wasn't your fault," my father said. "It was beshert. It was meant to be." With a heavy heart, I packed my trunk and set forth by train to an unwanted summer job.

When I saw the camp, I was impressed by its rolling green lawns and its location on a large lake dotted with small islands. But I still didn't want to be there.

The dining room I worked in was dank and dark, matching my mood. The wooden tables were lined up in rows, like soldiers at drill, which reminded me that I was just going through the motions. The children at my tables were the last to leave the mess hall after every meal and my station was the last to be cleaned. I had neither the desire nor the energy to be a waiter.

In my spare time, I ate. Working in the dining room was like putting a bull in a field of red flowers. I had free access to food and devoured any and all combinations, including peanut butter and cucumber sandwiches, apple pie and pickles and left over chicken and ice cream. I must have added ten pounds to my pudgy body and that was only in the first two weeks. I went back to my bunk at night and cried. I wanted my mother back. I wished I hadn't caused her death.

Several weeks later, I got a call from my father asking me to come home for a day in order to sign some papers to settle my mother's estate.

"Can't it wait until camp's over, Pop? I'm exhausted and need to rest on my day off this Thursday."

"The lawyer says these papers have to be signed within ninety days or we'll lose a significant amount of money. That's the end of next week."

"I'm too tired. Why don't you bring them up here and I'll sign them?"

"I can't miss work. Besides, there's a lot of paper-work and the lawyer has to explain everything to you."

My mother had died intestate and my brother and I had inherited one third each of some properties that for tax reasons were owned by my mother. My father needed us to sign our shares over to him so he could sell the property and use the cash for a new construction business he was starting. I was perverse and bent on giving him a hard time.

"I don't know if I can make it this week, Pop. Let's see how I feel."

"Look, I don't have time for this foolishness. I need you here on your day off. Do you understand?"

"Okay, Pop. I'll come home Wednesday after work. I'll check the train schedule, but it will be late. Don't wait up for me."

When I finished work Wednesday evening, I dragged my weary body to the train station and caught a local that would stop at every jerkwater town in Connecticut, before reaching New York City. I plopped myself into two facing seats and put my feet up. I stared out the window while munching on a Baby Ruth bar. I saw rows and rows of brightly lit apartment buildings as we approached a town, followed by tree after tree in full green foliage as we emerged back into the countryside. Soon I was sound asleep.

I woke up with a start as the train lurched to a stop in New Haven. I looked out the window and saw passengers scurrying to board other trains. They reminded me of ants trying to get down the ant hole. I wiped my eyes, yawned, and fiddled with some papers on the seat next to me. Had they been there when I sat down? I lifted them and saw they were a train time table. I noticed that if I switched to the express on the next track, I could be in New York a half hour sooner. I grabbed my bag and dashed across the platform, joining the other ants. I plopped myself into a seat and resumed napping.

We pulled into Grand Central Station and I caught the IRT subway to Brooklyn, exiting at Kingston Avenue. I trudged the five blocks to my house and was grateful it was late enough that I wouldn't have to deal with my father until the next day.

He woke me early in the morning and rushed me to the lawyer's office. I was having enough trouble dealing with my mother's death and had no desire to listen to the lawyer recite the options I had in regard to my mother's property. As he continued to talk, my face became warm and I rubbed my hands together. I wiped a tear from my eye. "Where do I sign?" I managed to say.

When we left the lawyer's office, my father took me out to lunch, but he had to return to work when we finished. I went to our house, looked at my mother's soup tureen, and cried. I was grateful that I would be on my way back to camp before my father's return. I was angry that he had put me through this ordeal, which seemed like rubbing salt into my wounds.

When I reached Grand Central Station, I learned that all trains were delayed. There had been a derailment the night before and the track hadn't been cleared, leaving one less track on which the trains could run. The lady at the information booth was surprised that I hadn't heard about it. "It's been all over the news," she said. "Last night's local crashed outside of Bridgeport. It jumped the track. A lot of people were killed or injured. That's why the trains are delayed tonight."

My God, I thought, that's the train I was supposed to be on. I didn't know if I would have been in one of the involved cars, but I was scared and started to shake anyway. I managed to board my train when it was called, two hours later.

The ride back to camp seemed to take forever and was slowed even further as the train crept towards Bridgeport. I stared out the window at the wreckage. Three or four cars were battered and twisted, like the licorice stick I was eating. I trembled and thought about how lucky I had been. Then I realized that this was what my father had meant when he used the Yiddish expression beshert. For some reason God had meant for me to live. I realized also it was beshert that my mother had to die. God must have had some reason for allowing that to happen too. I reached my hands toward the wreckage, touched the window and forgave myself.

As we left the park, I knew that if anything happened to Dotty, I wouldn't forgive myself. I knew this was as irrational as not forgiving myself for my mother's death when I was an adolescent. But as a physician, could I, should I, have done more now.

The next day we drove home. My mind kept jumping from the injured boy in the park, to my mother, to Dotty. When we got home, Dotty hugged Chuck, and we thanked him and Maureen.

The following week, we were back in Dr. Orgel's office to have the next round of chemotherapy. When we were in the back, and Dotty was having her IV inserted by the nurse, she looked around. "Oh my God, Liza's not here. I forgot to call or visit her since we got back from Disney."

The nurse overheard Dotty and started to stammer. "Didn't you know? Didn't someone tell you?"

"Tell me what?"

The nurse shook her head. "Liza passed away."

Dotty's face turned ashen. "What happened?"

"The infection got the best of her and in the end she bled into her brain. I know you two had become close. I'm so sorry."

Dotty shivered.

The nurse put her arm around Dotty's shoulder. "It's a very rare complication. It won't happen to you."

How do you know, I thought? How do you know Dotty won't suffer the same fate as Liza and my mother? I bent over and kissed the top of Dotty's head. "Everything will be okay," I said. Somehow, I didn't even sound convincing to myself.

Chapter Twelve

—Lenox Hill Hospital

Dotty's chemotherapy went off without a hitch. She didn't even lose a single hair. But Liza's death had taken its toll. Dotty had difficulty focusing. Often I had to repeat myself several times for her to remember what I had said. She became non-communicative and withdrew into a shell. I was sure she was punishing herself for not being more of a friend to Liza at the end, for enjoying herself at Disney while Liza was in the hospital, and for missing her funeral. My suspicion was that Dotty was contemplating her own mortality.

I tried to cheer her up, with little success. "Only two more sessions to go," I said. "Look how well you're doing."

"Liza was well until her last round of therapy."

"That's different."

"How so."

"First of all what happened to Liza is a very rare occurrence. Also Liza had a port which increased her risk. Maybe she was getting the stronger combination of drugs, or her disease was more advanced. Your situations aren't comparable."

"But what happened to her could happen to anyone, right?"

"Very, very, rarely. Why don't we focus on the good things, like our daughter being about to give birth to our second grandchild."

"Yeah, like that. I might not be able to go to New York when Ruth delivers, or even go to the bris if it's a boy."

"Let's cross that bridge when we come to it. You didn't miss going to Disney with Chuck, did you?" As I said this, I could have bitten my tongue.

Tears welled up in Dotty's eyes. "Look what happened while we were away."

I put my arm around Dotty. "You have to think positive. How many people have told you that's the key to success in beating this thing?"

Dotty stared at me with a blank expression on her face, as tears rolled down her cheeks.

Ten days later, we were in Dr. Orgel's office to have Dotty's blood work done. Her demeanor had remained morose, hope had been driven into despair. Forgetfulness had replaced a once sharp mind. I found her asking the same questions in an endless fashion. Ruth was to deliver in two weeks. I tried to be ebullient about it, without much enthusiasm on Dotty's part. It was the dead of winter, and a trip north during that time was never one of Dotty's favorite activities. Her present attitude magnified the situation. Still, if her blood parameters would allow her to travel, we planned to be there for the delivery, or at least go up afterwards, perhaps for a bris.

I sat with my arm around Dotty, listening to the ticking of the automated machine analyzing her blood. Where was the human element? Was the machine more accurate? Maybe, but the machine couldn't tell the difference between malignant and non-malignant cells. I was confident that in this situation it wasn't very important, but... I thought back to my days in medical school—to my time as a lab technician at Lenox Hill hospital in Manhattan.

At the start of my senior year, it looked like I would be a doctor, although the prospect didn't thrill me. I had gone through the torture of medical school to please my father and to keep the vow I had made upon my mother's death. I had passed all the required courses and had mainly electives left to take. In fact, my father felt secure enough that I would graduate, that he and my stepmother Susie, moved to Florida. We struck a deal before he left. He would buy me a car and I would get a job to pay for all expenses except tuition and books.

My father found a 1954 Chevy for $200 that his mechanic assured him was in tiptop condition. It was my first car and if I had realized how valuable this particular model would become, I might have treated it with a little more respect and spent more time babying it. But instead, my abuses, like not spending scarce money to change the oil, caused the car to perform sporadically at its own whim.

I found a job as a night lab technician at Lenox Hill Hospital, on the east side of Manhattan, a long way from medical school in Brooklyn. I had to do the preop blood work on patients scheduled for elective surgery the next day. The job provided a small stipend and an on call room to be used working nights. The room was undecorated and sparsely furnished with two single beds, a wooden dresser and a rickety desk. I made the room my primary domicile, while the other bed was used, on a rotating basis, by one of the three medical students from Flower Medical School with whom I shared the job. Each of us was on call every fourth night.

I had use of all the hospital facilities including the gym, but board wasn't provided except for the midnight snack. I stood on line, garnered four portions of tuna fish, eight slices of bread and extra plates of lettuce. At the table, I slathered the tuna on the bread, added the lettuce, wrapped the sandwiches in a napkin and squirreled them in my lab coat. This stash would provide my food for the next day.

I became friendly with one of the three Flower students who worked as night technicians. Fred had the same appearance as my cadaver, "Dead Fred." He was gaunt and had a pasty complexion. A mop of curly amber hair, heaped high on his head, compensated for his lack of stature. A broad smile seemed to be permanently pasted on his face.

One day, I asked, "How do you get the work done so fast? You're finished at 9:30. I'm in the lab until midnight."

"Just quick," Fred answered. "Besides, I love medicine and love what I do. It's fun for me."

I wondered if it was my incompetence or his superior mental and physical dexterity that enabled him to complete the work so much faster than I could. In fact, everything Fred did was fast. He finished a twenty page chapter in a textbook in the time it took me to read three pages. He gobbled a plate of food at the midnight buffet before I had put the napkin in my lap. He readily expounded in great detail about medical conditions that I could only vaguely recall.

"The other guys finish about the same time I do," Fred said. "You must be slow."

This certainly wasn't helping my feeling of inadequacy. "Can you give me some hints?" I asked.

"I'll bet you stain the God damn slides one at a time."

I nodded.

"If you stain them all at once, you won't have to wait for the stain to take on each slide before you can read them."

That sounded like a good pointer. The next night, I worked diligently in the lab, took Fred's advice, and finished a half hour sooner. It was still much longer than the time it took the other technicians to complete the work.

Several Sundays later, I received a call to draw some preop blood work from a lady on the V.I.P. floor. When I walked into the room, I saw a hatchet faced, heavily made up older woman, propped in her bed, wearing a robe trimmed at the collar and cuffs with fur. She talked French to her French attendant and German to her German maid. Looking up at me, she asked in heavily French accented English, "What do you want?"

"I'm here to do some preop blood work."

She frowned and nodded. "Be quick," she said, as she rolled the sleeve of her robe above the elbow.

I applied a tourniquet to her wrinkled arm and out popped a vein wider than a railroad tie. I trembled as I jabbed her arm and fished for the vein, but there was no blood return in the syringe.

"Out!" she yelled. "And send me someone who knows what he's doing." Then she turned to her French attendant and rapidly reeled off a series of animated phrases. Since I had many years of French in high school and college, I could make out the gist of her diatribe—something to the effect of, how dare they send me someone who doesn't know what to do?

I slunk out of the room and back to the lab. Since I was the only one on call, I really didn't know what to do next. The lady needed the blood work before she could have her gall bladder removed the next day.

I called Fred who lived in the neighborhood and asked if he would come by and draw the blood for me. "I'll be right there," he said.

Twenty minutes later, he delivered the blood to me in the lab.

"I really appreciate this," I said.

"No problem. See you at the midnight snack."

I took all the bloods that I had drawn that morning, numbered all the vials and corresponding slides, before making blood smears and reading them one at a time under the oil immersion lens of the microscope. This was boring, painstaking work and as far as I could tell, a pointless exercise. All the smears I had ever done were normal. The people they belonged to were only admitted for an elective surgical procedure, like a gall bladder removal or hernia repair. When I got to the fifteenth slide, I rubbed my eyes and started counting the different types of white cells. Something was wrong. Many of the cells seemed immature. In fact, there were blast cells, precursors to the mature white cells. I wondered if this patient had leukemia. When I matched the number on the slide to the person's name, I noticed it was from the French woman whose blood I had been unable to draw. I called her physician and reported my findings. He sent the head of pathology to look at the slides. He confirmed my suspicions.

"Good pickup, Paul," he said. "I'll talk to her doctor. They'll cancel the surgery."

I felt badly that the woman had a serious illness, but at the same time was elated that I had spared her needless surgery, and I was the one who made the diagnosis.

When I told Fred of my triumph that night, his usually ebullient smile vanished turning to a frown. He didn't congratulate me. After wolfing down his plate of pasta marinara, he got up to leave. "I'll see you tomorrow," he said. I couldn't understand his reaction.

The grinding of the machine spitting out Dotty's blood results caused me to refocus on her. She looked old, not because of her white hair, but because of her solemn posturing and deepening worry lines. I hoped hearing from Dr. Orgel that her results were normal would cheer Dotty up. He came in the room, looked at the paper and nodded. "A little lower, but nothing serious. You're good to go for the next round of chemo." I smiled, but Dotty's demeanor remained unchanged.

"Will I be able to go to New York for the birth of my grandchild?" Dotty asked.

Dr. Orgel knew that Ruth was due in two weeks. "Probably, but that will depend on when she delivers. If it doesn't interfere with your chemo and more important, if your blood parameters remain safe, you'll be able to go."

Dotty nodded. "I really want to go. For various reasons, we missed our granddaughter's birth. I want to be there this time."

"We'll see," Dr. Orgel said.

The morning before Dotty's fifth chemotherapy, we received a call from Ruth telling us she was in the early stages of labor. She asked if we were coming up for the delivery. I said, we'd love to, but mom is getting a treatment the next day. Ruth said she understood, but I sensed she was upset. After all, we had missed the delivery of her first child. Dotty got on the phone and I saw some animation for the first time in two weeks. "We'll come up in a week or so if all goes well and my blood work allows me to travel. If it's a boy, I'll do everything I can to be there for the bris."

Dotty listened for a few minutes and smiled. "I love you to, sweetheart."

"What did she say?" I asked.

"She's sure it's going to be a boy, so make sure we're there for the bris."

At two in the morning, the phone rang. Ruth's husband told us we were the proud grandparents of a healthy, baby boy. "I hope we can make it for the bris," Dotty said. "Tell Ruth I love her. I'll call tomorrow."

When Dotty hung up, I rolled over and grabbed her by the shoulders. "Wow!" I said.

Later that morning, on our way to Dr. Orgel's office, Dotty wasn't very talkative. "What's the matter?" I asked.

"I hope we can go to New York. I want to see Ruth, our granddaughter, and new grandson. I hope we can be at the bris."

"It's good to have hopes," I said. "Without them life is meaningless. If at all possible, we'll be there."

Dotty smiled for the first time in days. When we reached the office, I excused myself to go to the bathroom. When I came back, Dotty was chatting with a nervous looking woman who I took to be in her late forties. "This is Mary," Dotty said. "It's her first time here. I was just telling her how nice Dr. Orgel is and what to expect."

"Pleased to meet you, Mary." I shook her clammy hand. "The people here really are very nice. They'll make things as easy as possible for you."

Dotty continued whispering with Mary while we waited. I wondered if Dotty was thinking of Liza who mentored her on our first visit. I was glad Dotty had enough strength to return the favor.

As chance would have it, Mary was next to Dotty. They continued to chat and Dotty would interject what would happen next, to try and alleviate Mary's anxiety. We learned, like Liza, Mary was divorced and had lost her parents several years before. At least, she wasn't alone. A friend dropped her off and would be picking her up. Dotty sailed through her therapy without so much as a wave of nausea.

Before we left, Dotty looked at Mary whose thin face was puckered like a golf ball and had a greenish complexion. She walked over and put her hand on Mary's shoulder. "It gets easier," she said. "If you need anything, just ask." Then Dotty took out a piece of paper from her bag, jotted our number on it, and handed it to Mary. "Call me if you have any questions."

Good for you, I thought. You've had a good support system and now you're returning the favor. In a selfish vein, I'm sure that it will be helpful to you. In giving to others, you'll also be making yourself stronger.

At the door, Dotty stared at me. "What are you so pensive and smug about?"

I smiled. "Just thinking how beautiful you are."

"Yeah, sure."

We made reservations to go to New York two days before the bris, hoping Dotty's blood work would allow the trip. We spoke to our daughter every day. Mother and son were doing fine. Ruth told me to bring some numbing impregnated gauze to ease the pain of circumcision for our grandson. She didn't ask, but told me, as though she were expecting us to be there.

The day before we were to leave, Dotty went in for her blood work. I again sat listening to the ticking of the machine and watched it spew out the printout. As Dr. Orgel gave us the good news that Dotty's blood count was in the safe to travel range. I was already thinking back to my time at Lenox Hill Hospital, when humans transcended machines to get results.

The next day I got into the car, anxious to get to my internal medicine elective to tell my ex-roommate Marty about the great diagnosis I had made. I turned the key and even with a new battery the Chevy made a grinding noise before kicking over and starting. It had given up the ghost several times before I had replaced the battery. I drove down the East River Drive, past the United Nations building and through the haze that shrouded the lower Manhattan skyline, before going over the bridge to Brooklyn. Driving the length of Flatbush Avenue, I arrived at the Grand Army Plaza, and, under the large arch, the Chevy sputtered, stalled, and couldn't be restarted. I walked to a candy store, head bent to protect my face from the wind, called the AAA and waited for an hour while, shivering in the car. The tow truck arrived and pulled up head to head so that the mechanic could jump start the car. I stood between the two vehicles watching him apply the jumper cables. "Does this happen often?" he asked.

"About every ten minutes," I said facetiously.

He handed me his card. "When you get a minute, why don't you bring it into the shop?" As I nodded, the Chevy came out of neutral gear, lurched forward and mashed my shin into the bumper of the tow truck.

"Damn!" I screamed. I pounded my fist on the hood of the Chevy. "You're a curse." If my leg didn't hurt so much and wasn't impaled, I would have kicked a wheel or fender. The mechanic backed up the tow truck and I hobbled out.

"Are you okay?" he asked.

"I don't think anything's broken, but it really hurts. Maybe I'll go over to Kings County Hospital and get an X-ray."

I got into the Chevy which had started with the boost and drove to the emergency room. I felt guilty being taken out of turn because I was a med student, but was grateful. I was happy that the X-ray was negative, but by the time I was finished, I had missed my class and could barely walk because all the muscles in my shin had gone into spasm. I managed to get back to Lenox Hill Hospital by driving like my uncle Carl, the professional—one foot for the gas, the other for the brake.

The next day, I couldn't get out of bed because I was in agony. Fred was on call that night and when he finished at 9:30, he helped me to the shower and brought me food from the midnight buffet.

"If you can't work tomorrow," he said. "I'll take your shift and you can pay me back another time."

"Thanks," I said.

The next day, I was able to hobble, but couldn't work or go to school. The leg wasn't swollen or bruised, but each step caused me to grimace. I took Fred up on his offer. When he finished early again, I asked, "How the hell do you and the other guys do it?"

He winked. "We're just fast and efficient."

By morning, snow blanketed the area. I had missed two days of school and couldn't miss any more. Limping down to the Chevy, I prayed it would start, but if it didn't I had left myself plenty of extra time to get to class. To my surprise, it kicked over on the first try, and I had time to go to the cafeteria at Brooklyn Hospital, for a cup of hot tea, before making ward rounds.

When my day was finished, I hobbled through the snow drifts in the parking lot, turned the key in the Chevy's ignition and heard no response at all. After unsuccessfully trying a few more times, I pounded my head on the steering wheel. I had enough. I called my father's mechanic from whom we had bought the car and told him I didn't want it anymore.

"I'll take it off your hands and won't charge you for the tow. But I can't give you anything for it."

"Done," I said. The car was draining the small amount of money I earned. Besides, I could do without the aggravation. I tightened the hood on my parka, lowered my head into the driving snow and gimped to the subway.

Arriving back at Lenox hill Hospital, I shivered from cold and anger. What a bad deal I had made with my father. Not only wouldn't I have use of the car, but I would still have to scrimp to meet expenses.

Several nights later, I was on call again. My leg was feeling better, but still prevented me from moving at my usual pace, so I didn't finish in the lab until after midnight. After a quick snack, I fell into bed exhausted.

At 4 o'clock, of all nights, the phone rang. The operator informed me that I had a stat blood count to do. When I drew the blood from the patient, I realized it was a routine count for a young man who was to have a hernia operation at noon. It could easily have been done when the regular crew came to work, but the intern, who had forgotten to order the count, made it stat so he wouldn't be chewed out by his attending in the morning.

I was livid, but had no choice. Bleary eyed, I ran the hemoglobin, counted the white cells in the chamber under the microscope, stained the slide and tediously differentiated the types of white cells on the smear. As I worked, I seethed. This was just abusive, taking advantage of the lowest man on the totem pole.

When I finished, instead of calling the results to the ward, I got the attending's home phone number from the operator and called him, giving him the test results.

"Why the hell are you calling me with normal test results in the middle of the night?" he asked. "Are you out of your mind?"

"I'm sorry sir, but it was ordered stat and I thought it must be important enough to call you with the results." I said it calmly.

He slammed the receiver down and I limped back to my room, all the while smiling. I was sure the intern would get chewed out and wouldn't order routine tests on a stat basis anymore. Then I realized that the next year I would be an intern, working long hours, and felt badly about what I had done, but had no way to rectify the situation. When I got back into bed, I lay awake until it was time to go to school, but promised myself that I would apologize to the intern involved.

Several weeks later, it was still chilly outside, but buds were forming on the lilac trees heralding the imminent arrival of spring. Soon I would be finished with this job. I was working out in the hospital gym. Sweat poured from my body as I pedaled a stationary bike and then tinkered with free weights before trotting off to the sauna. When I finished it was 9 o'clock and I jumped into a shower.

After several minutes, I heard voices that I recognized. It was Fred and one of the other student technicians who was on call that night and had already finished work.

"You got done even earlier tonight," Fred said.

"It was a slow night and not counting the cell types on the slides really helps," Bill said. "Can you believe that Winick, he thinks we're fuckin' geniuses."

"Yeah, he's really gullible," Fred said.

I stood there shivering under the hot shower. No wonder they were finishing so much sooner than me. They were making up the results on the most tedious and time consuming part of the test, and were now having a good laugh at my expense.

Should I tell the pathologist in charge? It would have been my word against theirs and they all had seniority over me. I surely wouldn't be believed. I knew most of the counts were normal and were of no consequence to the patients' well being. But what about the lady with leukemia that I had diagnosed? Fred seemed so friendly. Maybe the night when he barely talked to me after I made the diagnosis of leukemia, he felt guilty that what he was doing could be potentially harmful? How could he be so dishonest? After my experience, how could he continue being so dishonest?

The next day, I saw the head of the lab, told him what I heard, and mentioned that if he didn't believe me, he could check out their work by repeating it himself the next morning. To my surprise, the pathologist wasn't angry and he thanked me for my honesty. He called the other students in for a talk. After that, Fred and his two classmates refused to speak to me anymore, and I was glad because I had no desire to speak to them. They weren't fired, but from then on, they didn't finish the pre-op labs until close to midnight.

It seemed ironic to me that I, who really didn't want to be a doctor, hated medical school and thought myself incompetent, meticulously did all the work, while Fred and his friends who professed to have a love for medicine, fudged the results. I wondered, if I was going to be a bad doctor, what kind of physicians would they be? Maybe I wouldn't be so bad after all.

"Paul, Paul, isn't that great news?"

"What? Oh yeah." I smiled. "Let's go home and start packing. Your results won't cause any worry."

"Yeah, right. I still can't get over what happened to poor Liza. Now I won't be available for Mary. Don't get me wrong, I'm dying to see my granddaughter and new grandson, but I feel guilty leaving and I'm frightened."

"You shouldn't. This should be a time of joy—a respite from this ordeal. An ordeal, by the way, I'm sure will have a happy ending." As I said this, I realized my mistake. That comment would only cause Dotty anguish.

"So now you're clairvoyant. Look what happened to Liza before her last dose of chemotherapy. Could you have predicted that? How do you know it won't happen to me.?"

"Because I know." We pulled into our driveway. "Now let's get ready to celebrate the birth of our grandson and have some fun." In my heart though, I knew we'd have no fun until Dotty's ordeal was over, and maybe not even then.

Chapter Thirteen

—Auntie Mame, Auntie Maverick

We flew to New York first class. It was the first time we had done that on a domestic flight. I knew it would please Dotty, particularly in her present state of affairs. We clinked wine glasses as we listened to the drone of the engines. "L'Chaim," I said.

"I hope it's to life, but . . ."

"What's the matter?"

"I feel guilty as Hell," Dotty said.

"Feeling pretty guilty about Liza?"

"That too?"

"What then?"

"I feel guilty because I caused this whole mess, you know, the breast cancer."

The flight attendant came by and gave us each some warm nuts. I waited until she left before replying. "You know, we've talked about this before. It's just not so."

"How can you say that? Didn't I make the decision to take hormone replacement therapy knowing estrogen can cause breast cancer?"

"First of all, estrogen doesn't cause breast cancer. There is only a very slightly increased risk of developing it if a woman uses estrogen. Don't forget you weighed the risk of hormone replacement therapy against the benefits." I took a sip of white zinfandel. "You lowered your risk for osteoporosis and you didn't have any hot flashes."

"Great decision, huh?"

All I could think of was a cliche. I put down my wine, faced Dotty and took her hands. "You've got to go with the hand you've been dealt. With the good medical care you've been getting, and a positive outlook on your part, you can make it a winning hand."

"How can you be so sure?"

I smiled. "I just am."

After we ate our mystery meat sandwich, we both closed our eyes. I wondered what Dotty was dreaming about? I wondered how I could help her alleviate the guilt she was feeling? Soon I had drifted off too. Flitting around me was my Aunt Lillian, nicknamed Lennie, better known to us as either Auntie Mame, or Auntie Maverick.

With Aunt Lennie it was always a love-hate relationship. If at a particular moment in time, you had incurred her wrath, she would chew you up and spit you out. If you were on her good side, the Auntie Mame persona would emerge. I always thought this was, to say the least, unusual behavior for a psychiatrist. But whatever she did, it was always done her way.

I was fourteen-years-old in 1951, when my brother applied to medical school. He had a good average from a first rate university, Columbia, but competition for acceptance was fierce. The Korean War raged and the number of applications had increased because students wanted to avoid the draft. It was almost a prerequisite for admission that an applicant would have someone on the inside pushing for his or her admission. My mother was counting on her sister Lillian to use her clout to get my brother into medical school. After all, she had used it for herself and her record was much spottier than my brother's, and her schooling was not as prestigious.

I often heard my mother talking on the phone to her sister. "Lillian, he still hasn't heard. Have you talked to Dr. Elway?" After my aunt replied, my mother responded. "Don't tell me not to worry. You know how difficult it is to get in now. You know it's my dream to see my boys become doctors. So please, do everything you can."

Several weeks later, my brother received notice of an interview at New York University. My parents were elated. "I told you that Lillian would come through," my mother said.

After the interview my father asked, "So how did it go?"

"Pretty well," my brother answered. "They didn't seem to want to give me a hard time, like in some of my other interviews."

Nodding, my father smiled. "It looks like you're going to get in."

The following month when my brother still hadn't heard, my mother called Lillian again. "Are you sure everything is okay? He's going to get in, isn't he?"

When she hung up my mother turned to my father. "Lillian says everything is set. He should hear soon."

Indeed, two weeks later, my brother got a letter from New York University. *I am sorry to inform you that despite your excellent record, we are unable to offer you a place in the entering freshman class. Competition has been very keen, and it took careful deliberation to arrive at this difficult decision. Good luck in your future endeavors.*

My mother was livid. She called up her sister. "How could you do this to me—to him?"

When Lillian responded that she had done her best, my mother screamed. "Like Hell you did." She slammed the receiver into the cradle. "I'll never talk to her again."

My parents thought that Lillian hadn't tried her best because she didn't want to be usurped as the only physician in the family. But for whatever reason, my aunt the maverick, had started a vendetta and would have it her way.

In November, we were driving my grandmother home after my father had shepherded her to a Hadassah meeting. My mother kissed my grandmother goodnight. "I'll see you at our house for Thanksgiving dinner."

My grandmother, who my father affectionately called the Chief, cleared her throat. "We're going to Lillian's. She invited us first."

"What do you mean, invited you first? You always have Thanksgiving dinner at our house."

The Chief just shrugged. I was sure she was punishing my mother for not talking to Lillian. She had sided with her younger daughter, and was convinced that Lillian had done all she could to secure my brother's admission. Despite my mother's protestations, the Chief wouldn't change her mind. Since the Chief had spoken, all her adult children followed suit. Lillian had extracted revenge. There was no crossing her.

My recollection of my aunt fast forwarded to her Auntie Mame persona. I was stationed in Biloxi Mississippi, at Keesler Air Force Base. I had arranged to go to New York to take a course in electromyography, as we had found a machine stored in the basement. It would be an aid in diagnosing muscle and nerve diseases in children. When we arrived, we called my Aunt Lennie and she invited us for lunch. By that time both my parents had died and Lennie's vendetta died with them. Lennie herself had married and divorced the same husband twice, and was now single after divorcing her third husband. Dotty and I went to Lennie's apartment on Central Park South, bringing our two-year-old son, Charlie (Chuck). She had made a ham for the occasion, which I ate with relish, since in my Jewish upbringing, it was never served in my house, or any of my relatives houses. When we finished lunch, I stood up to help clear the table, but Lennie put her hand up and looked at Dotty and me. "You two shoo. Get lost for the afternoon. Leave Charlie with me."

I glanced at Dotty and realized we hadn't been out since our son was born. Still, We were hesitant. "Will you two just leave," Lennie said.

We did as we were told, spending the afternoon at Radio City Music Hall. We saw the original movie of *MASH* and the Rockettes performing live. When we got back to Lennie's apartment there were hundreds of toys on the floor. They had bought out FAO Schwartz, and she and Charlie were sitting on the floor playing with his new acquisitions.

"I'll bet you didn't have as good a time as we did," Lennie said.

I smiled. "I bet you're right."

My recollection fast forwarded to a few months ago. Susie, Lennie's daughter, called to tell me Lennie had terminal lung cancer. "When, how?" I asked.

"She's had it for three years and chose not to tell anyone, including me. She decided not to undergo treatment and continued to smoke. You know my mom. She didn't want any interference. It had to be done her way."

I heard the quiver and resentment in my cousin's voice. "Is there anything I can do?" I asked.

"No, I just wanted you to know she's pretty sick and will probably die soon."

When I hung up, I called Lennie. Her speech was labored and raspy. "Don't grieve for me," she said. "I've lived a full life and did what I wanted to do, when I wanted to do it. I have no regrets."

I smashed the phone into the cradle when we were finished talking. I was angry that Lennie hadn't told anyone—that she wouldn't let me, my brother, or even her own daughter, all physicians, help. I was livid that she hadn't at least tried to lick the cancer. But I realized that was her decision not mine.

Dotty pushed me into real time. "Put your seat belt on. What have you been so pensive about?"

"I was just thinking about what you said. You know, about taking hormone replacement therapy and that causing the breast cancer." I saw Dotty's lips twitch. "You did it with good reason, incurring only a slightly increased risk. Aunt Lennie smoked packs of cigarettes a day knowing their potential harm, and then continued to smoke after she was diagnosed. Yet she has no regrets and continues to live life to the fullest. We'll probably see her at the bris if she's up to it."

I hoped Dotty had gotten my message. We held hands and she squeezed mine as the plane touched down on the runway.

We stayed at the Long Island Marriott near my daughter's house, so that we could go back and forth easily, allowing Dotty to rest. Ruth had warned me that our granddaughter had developed a phobia for men and I shouldn't take it personally if Martina didn't respond to me. We came into the house laden with gifts for the children. I saw Martina withdraw into a corner. Sitting on the floor away from her, I unwrapped some of the presents, laid them in front of me and played with them. I carried on a conversation with a teddy bear, explaining to it how one of the games worked. Martina inched closer. "You are a smart teddy to understand that game so fast."

"Show me too," Martina said.

"My pleasure." We played with all the toys and in a few minutes, my three-year-old granddaughter was sitting in my lap. When we finished, I took her two pudgy hands in mine. "How'd you like to go for a walk? Maybe we can do something special. I have an idea. Why don't we collect piles of wood and make stick piles in front of your house?"

Ruth rolled her eyes. I imagined she was thinking of the junk she would have to clean up when we left.

Martina and I strolled around the neighborhood picking up broken branches and depositing them on the front lawn. When we reached the mother load, a construction site, we carried pieces of lumber and deposited them on our pile. We were having such a good time that for the moment I forgot about Dotty and her ordeal. I was snapped back into reality when Dotty came to the front door. "I'm exhausted," she said. "Let's go back to the hotel so I can rest."

I couldn't imagine what exhausted her. She sat on the couch most of the afternoon, hardly interacting with her granddaughter. Everything had become an effort. I hoped that when her therapy was over, she would return to her pre-morbid, energetic state, but I was starting to have my doubts. I picked Martina up, brought her into the house, and gave her and Ruth a kiss. I turned to Dotty and stared. "Let's go to the hotel."

Dotty winced. Perhaps my voice was harsher than I intended. I resented being dragged away, since we would only be here for a few days. I turned to Ruth. "We'll see you tomorrow for the bris. We'll be here early. Can we bring anything?"

Ruth shook her head. "Just yourselves."

The next day, we arrived at Ruth's house an hour before the briss. Lennie was already there, having been taken by chauffeur driven limousine from Manhattan to Long Island. Her pale complexion, and stick like figure, blended into the white couch. Her breathing was rapid and her speech breathy. Despite her condition, Lennie's hair had been recently colored and was perfectly coiffed. She fidgeted with the fingers, as if searching for a cigarette.

I walked over and kissed her cheek. "How are you Aunt Lennie?"

"I'm okay, bubbeleh. How . . ." She paused to take a deep breath. "How does it feel to be a grandfather again?"

I smiled. "Great! I guess it's my reward for letting my teenager live."

She returned my smile. "I know what you mean."

I excused myself to go upstairs in order to wrap numbing gauze around my grandson's penis. It would take about forty-five minutes to take effect, just in time for the moyle to perform the circumcision. When I came back downstairs, Dotty was holding Lennie's hands, as they whispered together. "You two look like you're cooking up some conspiracy," I said.

Lennie smiled and beckoned me over. "Just reminding Dotty not to tell anyone about my condition. I'm doing fine—doing what I want to do. I don't want sympathy. Also, I'm trying to convince Dotty to live each day like it's the last. That's the attitude I've adopted." Lennie started to cough and hacked a piece of mucous into a tissue. "I just had to tell Dotty this because she looks so glum."

"It's not so," Dotty said.

Lennie put up her hand. "Let's not argue. Let's enjoy the celebration."

Lennie, being a psychiatrist, sensed Dotty was having a hard time. Lack of energy and a glum demeanor were clues even a lay person would have no trouble deciphering. Lennie had tried to share her experience with Dotty, but either the message wasn't getting through or it was being ignored.

The house was beginning to fill with family and friends diminishing our ability to talk privately with Lennie. At the circumcision, I noticed her hovering in the background. One life is ending, and a new one is beginning, I thought. When the moyle performed the circumcision, I winced, but my grandson didn't cry—the numbing gauze had worked.

After the bris, we did what Jews always do at any occasion, good or bad, eat. I stuffed a bagel with lox and cream cheese into my mouth, and looked for Lennie. She was tired and getting ready to leave. I went up and kissed her cheek. "Take care of yourself," I said.

"More important, take care of Dotty. I'll be fine."

Where did she get the strength, I thought. How can she be so glib about dying? Then I realized, she had lived long, and always did it her way. But I wasn't ready, perhaps because she was the last one of my mother's generation alive, and my generation would be next. It was partly because of Dotty's breast cancer. I could visualize Dotty in Lennie's position. I just wasn't ready for Lennie to die.

When the celebration was over, we stayed a little longer, then said our goodbyes. Dotty was tired and we had an early flight the next day. I kissed Ruth and congratulated her and her husband, Frank, for producing such a good looking offspring. "Thank God, he doesn't look like me," I said. I picked up Martina and whispered in her ear. "Thank you for making stick piles with me. You take good care of your mommy, daddy and baby brother. Remember, I love you."

She threw her arms around me. "I love you too, Papa Paul."

I wished they lived closer so that we could spend more time with them. Maybe at a later date they would, I thought. After all, Frank's mother was moving to Florida. Perhaps they would follow.

The next day, we flew back first class. The breakfast being served was either gloppy scrambled eggs or soggy French toast. I ate with relish, as usual, but Dotty just pushed the food around the tray. Her reaction was opposite from mine. She stopped eating when she was nervous.

"What's the matter?" I asked.

She shrugged.

"Come on."

"I'm scared of what's going to happen with the next round of chemo. I keep seeing Liza's face dancing in front of me."

"You have to get those thoughts out of your mind. You have to focus on the good things."

"I know, but . . ."

"Look at Lennie. She really is dying and is trying to live her life to the fullest. She dragged herself to the bris instead of wallowing in pity."

"What good is living life to its fullest, if you have no life to live."

I started to argue with Dotty, but thought better of it. Would this nightmare ever end? Would we get our life back the way it was? I had my doubts.

Chapter Fourteen

—Aruban Burial

When we arrived home, Dotty made a beeline for the phone to call Mary. I went into the bedroom, resentful that I was doing all the unpacking. As I finished, Dotty came into the room and pointed to the suitcases. "Thanks for doing that," she said. "I really appreciate it."

I shrugged. "How's Mary?"

"She says she's doing fine—no sign of fever or infection. Her white count was a little low so Dr. Orgel was just being cautious when he postponed her chemotherapy. We've arranged to meet in his office in two days, when we're both getting our blood work done. I hope my count is okay, so that I can have my last chemo session next week."

I nodded. "Everything is going to be fine."

Dotty pointed to the ceiling. "From your mouth to His ears."

"Maybe it's Her ears," I said.

Dotty smiled. "Whoever, as long as your prediction comes true."

I reached for her, but she shied away. "Let's have lunch," Dotty said. "I'm so tired that I think I'll take a nap afterwards."

On the day of the blood count, Dotty was apprehensive. She walked throughout the house searching for something. "What are you looking for?" I asked.

"My reading glasses."

"They're on your head."

She patted the top of her head, then hit her temples with the heels of her hands. "Stupid me."

I put my arms around her. "I told you everything is going to be fine."

Dotty stared up at me and shook her head.

When we arrived at Dr. Orgel's office, Mary was already there. She and Dotty whispered together. I heard very little of their conversation, but from what I did hear, I could guess as to what they were chatting about. I heard Mary say things like, I hope so, and later, please let it be true.

When Mary was called in for her lab work, I turned to Dotty. "What was all that whispering about?"

Dotty rubbed a tear that had formed in the corner of her right eye. "If you can do it, why not me? I told her everything will be okay. You're in good hands here."

When Mary came out, she had a smile on her face. My blood's okay. I'm going to have my second round of therapy tomorrow." She gave Dotty a hug. "Thanks for talking to me. See you tomorrow."

"I hope so."

When we were called into the lab, Dotty had her blood drawn and I listened as the machine clicked away. Was this impersonal chunk of metal and glass really more accurate than a human. Maybe, maybe not, but it certainly was faster. When Dr. Orgel looked at the printout, I thought I detected a twitch in his lips. He shook his head. "It's a little low," he said. "I think we should postpone the therapy until next week."

Dotty blanched.

"What's a little low?" I asked.

"The platelets are 43,000." When he said this, images of my mother lying in a coma floated in front of me. "And the white count is only 2,500 with an absolute neutrophil count of 1,100." With this latter bit of news, all I could think of was poor Liza who succumbed with numbers like those. At least Dotty didn't have any fever.

"How bad are those numbers?" Dotty asked.

"Really not too bad. I've seen much worse. But I just think it's safer to wait a week. Everything is going to be okay."

"That's what everyone keeps telling me," Dotty said.

"Try not to expose yourself to anyone that's sick. By next week your count should be up. We'll schedule the chemo for then, and repeat a count just before we start."

"I, I'm frightened," Dotty said.

"Nothing to be frightened about," Dr. Orgel said. "It happens all the time."

But it doesn't happen all the time to my wife, I thought. And there's nothing for you to be frightened about, since you're not the one with breast cancer.

"As long as you don't get sick or run a fever, everything should be fine," Dr. Orgel said. "Call me if anything like that happens."

Dotty nodded.

When Dr. Orgel left, I turned to Dotty. "We'll be careful this week, and stay mainly in the house."

"A lot of fun that'll be."

"At least, by the time we come back here, everything will be okay."

Dotty looked at me with a blank stare, opened her mouth to respond, but didn't utter a word.

During the week, each time Dotty said she was cold, hot, or had a minor ache, I cringed. Despite my apprehension, she did well—no infection, no fever. On Thursday, the day before Dotty's last chemo session, I received a call from my cousin Susie. From her tremulous voice, I could tell the news was not good. "Hi, what's up?" I asked.

"Mom passed away."

"I'm so sorry. She didn't look well at the bris. You were expecting it, weren't you?"

"Yeah," she answered. "But I guess you're never ready."

I thought about my parents, particularly my mother. "I know what you mean."

"Typical of my mom. Even in death, she wants to do it her way."

"How so?"

"She's going to be cremated."

"Jews don't get cremated."

"I know, but that's what she wanted. So what's the harm?"

"None, I guess."

"She wants to have the ashes scattered in the ocean in front of her house in Aruba. Will you do me a favor?"

Although Susie couldn't see me, I nodded. "Sure, if I can."

"You're going to Aruba to visit your brother in six weeks. Would you take the ashes down and scatter them as she wished? Maybe hold a small service on the beach for her Aruban friends?"

"Sure, but our trip is dependent on whether Dotty is up to traveling. By then, she'll be done with the chemo, so I think it will be okay."

"How is Dotty, by the way?"

I told my cousin what had been transpiring She tried to reassure me the way I had been reassuring Dotty. However, after Lennie's death, those assurances fell on deaf ears.

"We're having Mom's funeral in New York on Monday. I hope you can make it."

"I really want to, but that'll depend on Dotty's blood work, and how she tolerates the chemotherapy."

"The rest of the family is flying in from all over the country. I think mom would have enjoyed us having a reunion even if it was at her funeral. She was a real showman. Please try and come."

"I will try, but . . ."

"I understand. If you do come, would you say a few words at the service?"

"You bet. I really hope to be there. If there's anything else you need, let me know."

When I hung up, I wondered how to tell Dotty, or if to tell Dotty. She was in the bedroom resting. When I entered, her eyes fluttered open. "What's the matter?" she asked. "You look like you've seen a ghost."

"Susie just called. Lennie passed away." I told her everything my cousin and I had talked about. Dotty's dark complexion, which had been lightening because of an anemia caused by the chemotherapy, became paler.

"I want to go to New York, for the funeral," Dotty said. This surprised me. I expected her to beg off claiming fatigue, but she seemed adamant.

"You bet," I said. "As long as Dr. Orgel gives us the okay." I lay down next to Dotty, moistened the tip of my thumb, and wiped a tear from her eye.

The next day, we sat in the lab again listening to the clicks of the machine analyzing Dotty's blood. I hoped the results would allow Dotty to have the chemotherapy, and for us to be able to fly to New York for my aunt's funeral. But the thought of her numbers being low, caused images of my patients, friends, and family who had died from cancer, or bleeding problems, to flash before my eyes. I hoped Dotty didn't harbor any of these thoughts, and that she wouldn't join their ranks. When the machine spewed out the printout and Dr. Orgel came to give us the results, I felt my arms tense. I grabbed Dotty's hand. Dr. Orgel nodded. "Everything's great," he said. "Your numbers really increased. You're good to go today for your therapy."

"How high?" I asked.

"Platelets 93,000, white count 4,200'"

"That's great."

"We have a funeral in New York of my husband's aunt," Dotty said. "Will we be able to go?"

"When?"

"This Monday."

"If you tolerate today well, I don't see why not. Even if the therapy knocks the numbers down, it won't do it that quickly. Don't stay more then a few days, and come back in a few weeks to check things one more time."

Dotty and I both nodded. I hoped Dotty's premonitions about the last round of chemotherapy proved wrong. When the nurse jabbed Dotty's arm to start the IV, my arm ached. When she injected the Zofran to prevent nausea, I felt my nausea abate. With each drug coursing through Dotty's veins, I shivered. The good news however, was that Dotty sailed through the whole session without the slightest side effects.

When we left, Dotty turned to me. "I'm glad that's over. You may have been glib, but I was scared out of my mind."

"I know." Some glib, I thought.

"I have to do some shopping before we go to New York."

"What for?"

"I need a fancy hat to cover the gray hair, and to wear at the funeral."

I smiled.

"Now that my chemo's done, Dr Orgel says I'll be able to color my hair soon. Isn't that good?"

"If you say so. But to me, you're beautiful even with patriotic hair, red, white, or blue."

She smiled. "You're prejudiced."

"No, that's a totally unbiased opinion."

Later, I made reservations for us to fly to New York on Sunday morning, again springing for the extra money to buy first class tickets. In the meantime, I had to think about what to say at Lennie's funeral.

On the plane, I scribbled a few notes on a pad, outlining what I might say. I wanted my remarks to be unique—to highlight Lennie's Auntie Mame qualities, rather than her maverick dark side. I settled on recounting the FAO Schwartz episode where she had bought out half the store for Chuck. Surely none of my relatives would have a similar story to share.

Lennie's funeral was more a celebration of her life than a mourning for her death. What I hoped would be a unique story was one of many Auntie Mame stories told by my cousins and Lennie's friends. She was an equal opportunity Grande Dame to many people.

Dotty sat through the funeral with a somber demeanor, but did manage to smile at the stories and anecdotes being recited. I hoped Lennie's message to Dotty would emanate from her ashes. Life is meant to be lived to its fullest while you have the energy. There's no sense wallowing in pity—no sense living in fear of death. We're all going to die someday. In the meantime, enjoy life and your loved ones.

Indeed, Dotty's point about how can you live life to the fullest, if you have no life to live, had some validity. However, it was not true in Dotty's case, because at this juncture she was tumor free, and had a good prognosis. I hoped that now that her chemotherapy was over, she would snap out of the doldrums, and return to the once vibrant woman I married. But having cared for many patients with cancer, and having spoken to many parents who had cancers of their own, I realized the shadow of fear constantly flitted around them.

After the funeral, we went back to Lennie's apartment. The image of her sitting on the toy-laden floor with Chuck flashed in front of me. On a more somber note, seeing the rooms crammed with people stuffing their faces with food, reminded me of my house after my mother's funeral.

My cousin Susie took me aside. "How's Dotty?" she asked.

"Comme ci, comme ca."

"She seems so down."

"You know, the cancer, the mastectomy, the chemotherapy have all taken their toll. I'm glad it's behind us."

"Anything you need, let me know."

I smiled. "Back at you." We hugged.

"Thanks for coming today and for having the ceremony with mom's ashes, on the beach in Aruba," Susie said. "I'll mail them to you."

I nodded. "I hope it will bring you some closure."

"It will."

I wandered around the apartment sharing Lennie moments with anyone who would listen. When I saw Dotty, her back was to me. I put my arms around her and whispered in her ear. "I love you." She turned, buried her head in my shoulder, and we embraced.

Over the next four weeks, before our trip to Aruba, Dotty's solemn attitude remained. I tried to reassure her, tried to get her to think about our impending vacation, but all she could focus on was her cancer and what was coming next. She pointed to her chest. "I'm not looking forward to having this thing expanded. I hope it doesn't hurt. I dread thinking about going back every week, and having him inject salt water into this expandible, prosthetic breast, so that my chest will expand, and there will be room for the permanent implant."

I flicked both wrists back and forth. "Yeah, but then you'll have your beautiful shape back."

"Yeah, but not before I have another operation to replace this expander with the permanent new part of me."

"Let's not think of that right now. This afternoon, we have to go and get what I hope is your final blood count, and then get ready for our trip to Aruba next week. Let's not worry about the other stuff until we get back."

"Easy for you to say."

I guess it was easy because, it wasn't me who was going to have the painful stretching of my chest wall tissue, and then have my body invaded again. "I know," I said.

When we arrived at Dr. Orgel's office for Dotty's blood work, Mary was just leaving. She and Dotty stopped to chat while I registered. I could tell from the smile on Mary's face that things were going well. When Mary left, I turned to Dotty. "She's in a good mood."

"Yes indeed. Her blood work has been fine. She completed her third round of therapy without a hitch, and best of all, her close friend had a lump removed from her breast that proved benign."

"That's great." Why couldn't your lump have been benign, I thought? We went into the lab, and after Dotty's blood was drawn I listened to the familiar ticking of the machine—as familiar as the ticking of the clock on our living room coffee table, the clock we had won at a charity event to support ths Susan G Komen Breast Cancer Foundation. When Dr. Orgel gave us the results, I was ebullient. All of Dotty's lab work was back to normal, we were cleared to go to Aruba, and miracle of miracles, he didn't want to see her for three months. The corners of Dotty's lips tried to smile, but only moved a few millimeters. I guessed she was thinking of the road ahead, rather than the success of the road already traveled.

On the trip down to Aruba to visit my brother, I put Lennie's ashes in our carry on, not wanting to lose them if our checked luggage was misplaced. It gave me an eerie feeling having my aunt in a bin above my head. Our landing was smooth. I hoped this was an omen that we would have a smooth vacation, a smooth ashes scattering ceremony, and most important of all, smooth sailing for the rest of Dotty's breast cancer ordeal, including no recurrences.

On our way to the beach for the ceremony, I looked at the barren island—as barren as a woman without a uterus trying to conceive. The only vegetation were windblown divi divi trees, and rows of cactuses. Only in front of the hotels was there grass, flora, and foliage. Goats wandered aimlessly over the roads. The beach in front of Lennie's house had a rocky coastline, almost unsuitable for swimming. My brother had told all her friends about the service, but only a few attended. I guessed in Aruba, they saw her mean maverick personality more than her Auntie Mame one. The windy, barren island that is Aruba fit that image. My brother and I said a few words, then scattered the ashes. Waves along the rocky coast seemed to be pushing them back toward us, but at last they were no longer visible, having been swallowed by the ocean's undercurrents.

As the few people left, Dotty and I lagged behind. The two of us continued staring at the ocean. I put my arm around Dotty who was shivering from the wind and the emotion of the moment. "I don't want to end up like Lennie," she said. "I really don't"

Words stuck in my throat before I answered. "You won't." I said. "You really won't

Chapter Fifteen

–Jean's Jewels

When we returned from Aruba, our lives were filled with mundane, everyday tasks. Dotty was too busy to be upset. But as her appointment with the plastic surgeon neared, she became more and more agitated. She pointed to her chest. "I really don't want to have this expanded. The plastic surgeon said we'd have to come six or seven times, have saline injected so the tissues would stretch to make room for the permanent implant. It'll probably hurt like all get out. Then, it has to be taken out surgically and the new one put in. What the Hell for?"

"You said you wanted it done so you would look like a woman."

"Who cares?"

"You know, you do."

"What do you mean?"

"If appearance wasn't so important to you, why'd you go through the agony of two plastic surgical procedures, to have your nose done and your face lifted?"

"That was then. Now is now."

"Are you sure?"

She shrugged.

"You could wear a prosthesis to fill out the space when you go out."

Dotty's lips curled downward. "All these choices. Just too much. First, should I have a lumpectomy with radiation or a mastectomy? Then should I have any chemotherapy and if so, what kind? Now this. She wiped the spittle from the sides of her lips, and put her hands on her chest. "I guess I'll go through with it."

Knowing her penchant for maintaining her beauty, I realized this was the decision she would come to—that she was just venting. All the same, if these procedures caused her an inordinate amount of discomfort, or if she wasn't happy with the results, I didn't want to be blamed. "I hope you're not doing this for me. You're beautiful just the way you are."

She stared at me and hesitated before speaking. "No, for me."

I wrapped my arms around her and we embraced.

Several days later, we arrived in the plastic surgeon's office, filled out the requisite forms and waited. Forty minutes later, we were still waiting. I had leafed through three magazines familiarizing myself with all the back door dealings in the sports world, and Dotty just sat stoically, glaring at the receptionist's window. She jabbed me in the ribs. "Do something. I can't sit any longer."

I stuck my head through the window and asked what was happening. At first the receptionist didn't respond, continuing to push papers around her desk. "Did you say something?" she asked."

"No one has been called yet. Is there a problem?"

"Dr Lipton was delayed in surgery. He just came in. He'll be with you in a few minutes."

How many times had I heard a theme and variation of that line? I told Dotty what the receptionist said, and sat back down to flip more pages in a magazine. Ten minutes later, we still hadn't been called. Dotty shifted from side to side, and then stood up. "I'm going to the bathroom," she said.

I stared at the sign above the receptionist's window. *Donald Lipton, MD, Plastic Surgeon.* I knew that many plastic surgical procedures were invaluable, such as cleft lip and palate repair, but I never could fathom cosmetic surgery. I was against Dotty's previous cosmetic surgeries, but ultimately the decision had been hers. One day I asked her, "Why are you trying not to look like the woman I fell in love with?"

She answered, "Wrong, I am trying to continue to look like the woman you fell in love with."

I knew that many women felt that way and were insecure, trying to fend off their husband's roving eye for a younger woman. I hoped that wasn't true in Dotty's case, but despite her protestations, I was sure that at least had to be in the back of her mind. Now that she's facing breast cancer and her own mortality, how insignificant these decisions must have been, at least to me and I guessed to her. I thought about the mother of a patient of mine, and wondered if she had trepidations about her cosmetic surgery. I remembered meeting her in my local Publix supermarket ten or fifteen years ago.

As I walked down the aisle looking for Prego Spaghetti Sauce, I took a sideways glance at a blue-eyed, blond beauty. My gaze lingered longer. I tried to convince myself it was because of some recognition on my part. But even though I am a physician, and expected to exhibit more self control, I realized my actions were those of a typical lustful male. After I passed, her voice boomed. "So Dr. Winick, aren't you going to stop and say hello?"

I turned around, furrowed my brow and stared. "Hi," I said.

"You don't recognize me, do you?"

"You look familiar, but . . ."

"Jean, Jean Emmons."

I hadn't seen Jean for awhile, but thought I knew her appearance well. I had taken care of her teen-aged son, Joey, for years. I saw a slight resemblance but this didn't look like the same woman. Jean had brown hair, a fuller figure, an elongated nose and less endowed breasts. "You look different."

"Better, I hope."

"You bet. But how did you do it?"

"A change of hair style and color. A little nip here, a little tuck there." She pointed to her breasts. "A little addition there."

"Wow," I said

"You like, huh?"

"I like, but why?"

The smile on Jean's face turned to a smirk. "When my husband left me for a young bimbo, I was determined not to let that happen again. I wanted him to eat his heart out. It worked, but when he begged to come back, I told him to stick it,"

As a pediatrician, my first thought was of her son. "Is the divorce affecting Joey?"

"Not much. He's off to college next year, and will be pretty much on his own. In fact, I have to make an appointment in a few months for his college physical."

"Wow, time really flies," I said. "I remember when he was born."

"Time may fly, but I'm determined to push back. The new me is enjoying life."

"Well good for you. See you in a few months then."

As I walked away, I thought about how stunning she was, but was it really worth it? Maybe as a magnet for attracting males, it was worth it to her. However, in my mind, even though it was always nice to have an attractive book cover, it was the contents that mattered.

When Dotty returned from the bathroom, we were escorted to an examining room where we waited for Dr. Lipton. The walls were covered with pictures of women before and after they had either a breast augmentation procedure or nasal reconstruction surgery. I chuckled when I noticed they were smiling and dressed well in the after pictures, compared to being frumpy and frowning in the before pictures. Did they feel better about themselves? Maybe short term, but could it really make a big difference in their lives. Somehow, I doubted it.

Dr. Lipton came in and asked Dotty how she was doing. "Okay, I guess," she said. "At least I'm done with the chemo." Then she pointed to her chest. "I'm not looking forward to this business."

"Everything will be fine," he said. "Just a little discomfort. In the end, you'll love the way you look."

"I hope so. Tell me again why I can't have a silicone implant that looks more natural, rather than a saline one."

"The FDA took silicone breast implants off the market. Some question of side effects—fatigue and more serious stuff."

"That's right," Dotty said.

"But saline implants really do look just as good."

Dotty shrugged and then nodded.

Dr. Lipton drew ten ml. into a syringe and attached a long, thin needle. He opened the paper gown that Dotty was wearing, His fingers fiddled all over her chest, looking for the button on the temporary implant where he could inject the saline. Finally, a look of victory appeared on his face. "There you are," he said. He poked the needle through Dotty's skin and started injecting the saline.

Midway, Dotty wriggled on the table. "Ow that hurts."

I squeezed Dotty's hand.

"Just a little more," Dr. Lipton said. Dotty continued to grimace as the last of the saline entered the implant. Dr. Lipton took measurements of Dotty's remaining breast. "I have to order the permanent implant and I want to get an even match."

"I would think so," Dotty said. Sarcasm was not her thing, but in this case it spewed out. "I hope after going through all of this, the least you can do is leave me with a matched set."

"Don't worry, I will."

When he left, Dotty got dressed and kept rubbing her chest above the implant. "It hurts." she said.

"As the tissue stretches," I said. "It will get easier and easier." At least I hoped it would.

We made an appointment for two weeks to repeat the process. In the interim, I told Dotty, there was nothing for us to do but live and enjoy life. I believed this, but was it true?

Four days later, we were eating dinner when Dotty grabbed her chest. "It really hurts. Even more now."

I thought Dotty was being hypersensitive, so I nodded, and took a bite of macaroni and cheese. "I'm sorry," I said.

"The area's turning red. Is that normal?"

Dotty had my attention now. I finished chewing, put down my fork, and washed my hands. "Let me take a look."

Dotty unbuttoned her blouse, and indeed the area around the button was red—not flaming red, but pinkish, and it hurt Dotty when I touched it. "I think it's a little infected," I said. "Not bad, but you should call Dr. Lipton. In the meantime, I'd soak the area with warm compresses and put on some of the antibiotic ointment you have."

Dotty frowned and fought back tears. "Everything will be fine," I said. This was probably true, but I could see that no way were we going to be able to live life normally—not now, and I wondered if this dreadful disease with all its ramifications would ever allow us to.

Dotty called Dr. Lipton who agreed with what I had said, and also called in a prescription for another antibiotic to our pharmacy. He said she should come in if the area hurt more, became redder, or she developed a fever. Also, it would be wise to wait an extra week before coming in for further expansion treatments.

Fortunately, all went well. The pain and redness gradually subsided, and Dotty was able to keep her next appointment with Dr. Lipton. Again, the wait was interminable. I ploughed through magazines I hadn't scanned the last time, and from the corner of my eye saw Dotty squirming in her chair. As I was about to go to the desk again, we were called back. Dotty sat on the examining table, having changed into a paper gown, while I fidgeted in an uncomfortable chair that had been placed in a corner. We were lost in our own thoughts. My mind focused on Jean, and the time she brought Joey in for his college physical.

As they entered my office, Joey and I high-fived. "Way to go my man," I said. "Princeton, wow!" He smiled, but Jean's facial expression remained unchanged—kind of dour. It matched her looks that were different from what I had seen in the supermarket. Her face was pale and void of makeup. Her disheveled long hair lay limp on a crumpled blouse that revealed no cleavage. Certainly this was not the new look that she told me she was going for when we had last met.

"Are you okay?" I asked.

She nodded. "Just tired. Joey's college tour was a whirlwind and really exhausted me."

"It was worth it, I guess. Look where he's going."

"I really am proud of him. Money will be tight, but with student loans, we'll get by. Maybe his deadbeat dad will contribute something."

"Mom," Joey said. "You know he's about to get married again and he just lost his job. He'll do what he can. I'll work this summer and get a part time job at school. We'll be fine."

Jean raised her voice "Stop defending him."

Before Joey could respond, I jumped in. "Let's not argue. This is supposed to be a happy time."

Joey handed me the forms to fill out. "Let me examine you first. Do you want your mom to step out?"

"We have no secrets."

For the first time, Jean cracked a smile. As I performed Joey's physical, I glanced at her. She kept rubbing the right side of her neck. When I was finished, and had filled out the requisite paperwork, I looked up. Jean was still fiddling with her neck. "Something bothering you?" I asked.

"Not really. Just this knot I found. It doesn't hurt, but my shirt rubbing on it irritates me."

"Mind if I look?"

"Be my guest."

I felt an enlarged lymph node in back of the large muscle in her neck. It was firm, non-moveable and non-tender. It could be an infection, I thought. Maybe atypical TB or cat scratch disease, but I was concerned that it might be cancer. As a pediatrician, not responsible for Jean's care, all I could do was advise her to see her doctor. I had his name in my chart, and made a mental note to call him.

"So what do you think?" she asked.

"Probably nothing serious. Perhaps an infection. You really ought to see your doctor though, and make sure it really is nothing."

"You're freaking me out."

"Hey I take care of kids. Even with your new look, you're a little out of my age group." I smiled and put my hand on her shoulder. "But you really should get it checked out." I was hoping she had gotten my message without being scared out of her mind.

Joey chimed in. "Listen to Dr. W, mom. I'm sure everything will be okay."

"I will."

I turned my attention to Joey, and handed him the finished forms.

"Thanks, doc," Joey said.

I playfully punched him on the arm. "I'm really proud of you."

I turned to Jean. "Congratulations to you too. It has to be gratifying to have brought up such a fine young man. I pointed to my neck. "Don't forget to get that checked out."

When Dr. Lipton came in, Dotty verbally assaulted him. "When you inject that garbage into the implant, it's not going to give me an infection again, is it? Because if it does, I'm out of here. I'll just have the damn thing taken out."

Dr. Lipton, to his credit, didn't get angry. "No it was a rare occurrence and shouldn't happen again." He palpated for the button on the prosthesis, finding it easily this time. As he injected the saline, Dotty winced, but said nothing. "That should do it," he said. "I'm sure everything will be fine this time, but if you have a problem call me."

"You bet I will," Dotty said.

"See you in a few weeks."

As she got dressed, I thought is all this really worth it. I thought about Jean, and wondered, in retrospect, how she would have felt about all those cosmetic procedures she had undergone.

"Let's go home," I said. "Wine and dinner on me."

Dotty smiled. "You've got a deal."

Chapter Sixteen

–Reconstruction

There weren't any complications to the remainder of Dotty's implant expansions. This provided her some comfort, but as the time neared to replace the expander with a permanent prosthesis, Dotty became agitated. "I don't want to go through this anymore," she said. "I've had enough of surgery, chemotherapy, and being manipulated." She touched her chest. "I think I'll just keep this."

I shook my head. "You asked Dr Lipton about that. He said that would be unwise because it might leak, or become lopsided. I know you don't want that."

Dotty shrugged. "So what? If any of those things happen we could replace it then."

"That sounds more reasonable than the reality of the situation. If it does leak and we take it out, you'd be without anything for awhile, until things settled down in your chest. In the meantime, all the muscles might become tight and you'd have to start this whole process all over again. Your surgeon advised you to do this. Like you, I wish you hadn't started. But at this point, you may as well take it out sooner than later, and as long as you're having the surgery, you may as well have the permanent one put in. It won't prolong the procedure much."

"Why? Because I won't look like a woman to you?"

"Of course you will. But if you let Dr. Lipton change them, you won't have to deal with an external prosthesis to fill one side your bra. I just think it will be pleasanter for you."

Dotty kept shaking her head. "Damn, Damn, Damn."

"Hey, it's up to you," I said. "I'll support any decision you make."

Dotty clung to me and looked up into my face. "I guess you're right. I'll go through with it. I'm just nervous."

"Don't be. I'm in this with you for the whole ride."

I hoped this procedure, which Dr. Lipton dubbed minor, went off without incident. If it didn't, I knew that Dotty would blame me. Even worse, I would blame myself after everything I had just said.

The day before her surgery, we were in Dr. Lipton's office to get final instructions, and to have any last minute questions answered. While waiting, I leafed through two new magazines he had acquired. There was an ad depicting a flat chested beauty stuffed into a wonder bra. Why was there so much focus on the female breast as a thing of beauty? It all seemed so unimportant now. I hoped this procedure would be the last, and would put a happy exclamation mark on what had otherwise been a nightmare. But somehow, I doubted it. We had already spent some emotionally traumatic hours in preparation for this procedure. We waited at our internist's office so he could clear Dotty for surgery, and then waited again at the hospital to see the anaesthesiologist, and to preregister.

When we were called back to see Dr. Lipton, he flipped through her chart. "All set to go," he said. "Do you have any questions?"

"Yes," Dotty said. "Do I really need to do this?"

He smiled. "We've been through this."

"I know. Just hoping you changed your mind."

"See you tomorrow then."

That evening, Dotty had trouble falling asleep I lay awake with her, trying to provide some comfort, until we both passed out. In my dreams, I saw Jean. I was visiting her in her hospital room.

While walking through the hospital the smell of antiseptic, which always hovered there, intensified as I approached Jean's ward. When I entered her room, she was dozing. The pristine white sheet covering her body matched the complexion of her face. Gone was the recently created beauty. Her blond hair had become sparse, and was streaked with strands of gray. Her face lift was marred by deep grooves. Lack of makeup, intensified her ghost-like image. Not wanting to disturb her, I started to leave.

"Dr. Paul," she said. "Thanks for coming to visit me."

I smiled. "How are you?"

She shrugged. "You know, you started all of this."

"Me?"

"Yes, you. Remember when I brought Joey in for his college physical, you felt the lump in my neck?"

I nodded, but couldn't suppress a frown, because I knew what she would say next.

"They found an aggressive lymphoma—stage four. The chemo blew my white count to smithereens. That's why I'm in the hospital."

"A wise precaution."

"I want to thank you," she said.

"For what?"

If you hadn't pushed me into getting it checked out, I wouldn't be here today, and I wouldn't have any hope." She ran her fingers through her hair. "I must look like a real mess."

I shook my head. "Are you kidding? You look terrific."

She smiled. "You lie with a straight face. If I knew you were coming, I would have put on some makeup and brushed my hair."

Even with all she was going through, maintaining her beauty was important to her. Telling her that a male still found her attractive might give her a psychological boost, and I hoped at some level that better self esteem might give her immune system a kick start.

"Is there anything I can do for you?" I asked.

She shook her head

"A book, or something from the cafeteria?"

"No, I'm fine. Joey is keeping me well supplied."

"Speaking of Joey, how's he doing?"

Jean rubbed her eyes. "Not too well. Despite my protests, he's postponed going to college. Princeton granted him delayed admission until next year's class."

"That's certainly good."

"He wanted to stay with me. But with me not being able to work, I don't see how I'll be able to afford sending him."

"His dad won't help?"

"Yeah, sure. But at least the bum is spending more time with his son."

"That's certainly good."

"I guess."

We continued to chat, but her eyes were opening and closing, so I excused myself. As I was leaving, Joey arrived for a visit. We lingered in the hall to talk.

"How are you doing?" I asked.

"How should I be doing? My mother has cancer, is in the hospital, and might die. I've had to put off going to college. Mom's not working, so there probably won't be enough money for me to go to Princeton, and I've had to cut back my hours at the restaurant to help take care of mom. Everything's just peachy."

I'd never known Joey to use sarcasm like that. His mom's ordeal was obviously taking a toll on him. "How's dad?" I asked.

The corners of his mouth lifted, unveiling a faint smile. "That's one good thing. We're spending more time together—just hanging out."

I put my arm around him. "If you want to talk or need a sounding board, you know you can pop by the office anytime. Maybe we could even do lunch if you have the time."

"Thanks, I'll keep that in mind." He excused himself to visit with his mom.

As I left the hospital, I prayed for Joey and Jean. At best, hard times were ahead—at worst devastating times. Unfortunately, I sensed her fascination with looks wouldn't make any difference in her recovery. Just maybe though, it would provide her with some comfort.

On the morning of Dotty's surgery, I walked into the kitchen to wash down a potpourri of vitamins with a glass of orange juice. Dotty was there pouring Cheerios into a bowl. "Stop!" I said. "You know you're not supposed to have anything to eat or drink before surgery."

She tapped the side of her head. "I forgot. It's still dark out. I'm not awake yet."

I reached across the counter and kissed her. "Now, let's get ready."

At the hospital, we sat in the entry area and did what by this time we had become used to, and that is wait. I had hoped that a former patient of mine would again be at the registration desk and be able to expedite the process, but we had no such luck. I went through my routine of flipping through magazine after magazine without reading a word. When we were finally called, all the receptionist did was confirm the information we had put on the preregistration sheets. Then she sent for transportation to wheel Dotty to the surgical holding area.

"Why can't she just walk?" I asked. "She's not a cripple."

"That's the policy, sorry."

By the time the wheelchair arrived the sun had risen and was shining brightly through the windows. I hoped our life would get back to that same intense glow, but first we'd have to get through this moment.

We waited some more outside the holding area until the nurse took us back. I felt myself getting angry as she asked some of the same inane questions that had already been asked and answered. When she finished, Dotty changed into a hospital gown, was placed on a stretcher, and wheeled to a minuscule cubicle framed by two faded white curtains. I should have been used to this by now. Dotty had gone through similar machinations on the day of her mastectomy. Somehow, knowing what to expect and being prepared for it were as foreign to me as drinking an ice cream soda while eating Chinese food.

After Dotty was jabbed with a needle to start the IV, and chest leads were placed and hooked to a monitor, we did what was becoming more and more familiar to us, but something I would never get used to, and that is wait. Dr. Lipton's first case was taking longer than had been expected was the message relayed from the operating room, to the nurse, to us.

"Damn," Dotty said. "Why does this always happen?"

"Just to aggravate you." I held up my hand. "Just kidding."

"Well it's not funny."

"I know, sweetheart. I'm sorry. I don't like this either, but what can we do? Want to play geography?"

"You really want to aggravate me, don't you. Why would I want to play that? You know all of those stupid little countries and their capitals."

I smiled. "Maybe you'll learn something,"

"Yeah, sure."

I continued this inconsequential banter, hoping to distract Dotty—to keep her mind from focusing on the wait and the impending surgery. With this tactic, I had some success. She only complained a little during the next hour, before they came to wheel her into the operating room.

I kissed her forehead and gave her the thumbs up sign. "I'll see you in post-op in a little while. By then, this will be all over and everything will be fine."

She smiled. "I hope so."

I walked to the surgical waiting area, stopping to pick up a doughnut and a diet coke. As I sat there munching, a rerun of General Hospital was blaring on the TV. I closed my eyes and vague images of Jean flitted through my mind.

I was standing in an open area in the back of a crowd. Jean's family were up front, under a canopy. Joey was standing next to his father who had his large hand around his son's shoulder. Rain cascaded from the umbrella I was holding, landing in a small puddle at my feet, where it formed ever increasing concentric circles. Rain also dripped off the canopy, drenching a freshly dug mound of earth. A worm wiggled and writhed in an effort to maintain itself on the mound's crest, trying to continue its existence.

The rabbi chanted the Kaddish prayer. "Yisgadal, v'yiskadash shme rabor . . ." Joey rocked back and forth on the balls of his feet as Jean's body was lowered into the ground. When the rabbi had finished his eulogy, he handed Joey a shovel. He took a scoop of earth from the mound, as is tradition, and flung it into the grave. I noticed on this particular shovel full was the worm I had been observing.

Jean had passed away despite aggressive chemotherapy—despite being on a new experimental protocol. I visited her several times during the final days and was saddened to see her body shrivel. Her surgically enhanced beauty had been drained from her like the juice of a grapefruit being squeezed from its rind. I felt sad that she didn't have much time to reap the benefits of all that cosmetic surgery. I knew though, whatever time she had with her new features provided her with deep satisfaction. Was it worth it? Not for me to say.

Later, I stopped by Joey's house to make a condolence call. The mirrors were covered and he sat with his father on a hard bench. The dining room table was laden with food—bagels, lox, cream cheese and various salads.

Before leaving, I took Joey aside. "Have you given any thought to what you're going to do?" I asked.

"I'm going to move in with dad. He's going to put his wedding on hold for awhile,'

I nodded. "That's great! What about school?"

Joey stuttered before answering. "Mom was a special lady. She wanted me to go to Princeton and I'm going to start in the fall. Dad has a new job and is going to help. I'll get a part time job, student loans and apply for student aid. It won't be easy, but I'm motivated"

I smiled and grasped Joey's shoulders. "If you need anything, or want to talk, call me."

"I will"

Outside, racing through the rain to my car, I thought about Jean. I was sure she'd be happy to know that her deadbeat ex-husband had stepped to the plate. I hoped the worm I had observed at the funeral would work its way to the top of the grave.

I opened my eyes when the receptionist in the waiting room tapped my shoulder. "Your wife's in the recovery room," she said.

I rushed down the hall to Dotty. When I entered the recovery suite, Dotty was still groggy. Dr. Lipton was still there. "How's she doing?" I asked.

"Great! It should be easy sledding from here."

When Dotty came out of the anaesthesia, I kissed her forehead. "It's over," I said. "No more chemo, no more surgery. It's time to start living our lives and enjoying them like the best of times is now."

She smiled. "I hope so, but . . ." Her eyes fluttered shut, since she was still a little woozy from the anaesthesia. I thought about the worm in Jean's grave. I hoped that it had indeed reached the top—that in a sense this would symbolize a rebirth for us. But my doubts were magnified by Dotty's reaction of finishing happy endings with a but. I couldn't help visualizing the worm wiggling in the center of the grave, struggling to move upward.

Chapter Seventeen

–Biopsy

In the ensuing year and a half, Mary, like Dotty, had completed her chemotherapy and was now cancer free. They had kept in close phone contact and occasionally went out to lunch. After one such meal, Dotty came home sporting a Jack-O-Lantern smile. "What are you so happy about?" I asked.

"Mary's doing very well, and best of all, she's found someone. They're totally in love and are making plans to get married. Isn't that great?"

I nodded. "That is great. Clear sailing for the two of you from now on."

Dotty raised her hand extending an imaginary glass. "I'll drink to that."

We clinked fists.

About two months later, when I came home from some never ending business meeting, Dotty was on the phone. Her complexion was the color of chalk. Her free hand fiddled with her hair. When she turned around and saw me, I noticed tears in her eyes.

"What's the matter?" I asked.

She put up her index finger beckoning me to wait a minute. I listened as she continued to talk.

"Maybe it'll be nothing," Dotty said. Just a benign tumor like your friend Donna."

She listened for a minute, while bouncing on the balls of her feet. "I know you're more likely to have another cancer because you had one. But my husband always uses some silly baseball cliche that I think is very appropriate now. 'It ain't over till it's over.' Don't think the worst. I'll go with you for the biopsy. Think positively."

When she hung up, Dotty threw her arms around me and clung to my shoulders. She looked up at me. "You heard?"

I nodded. I was sure Dotty had mixed feelings—sadness for Mary, but guilt at thinking there but for the grace of God go I, and relief that it wasn't her. "Take your own advice," I said. "Stay positive. That's the best way to help Mary."

Two weeks later, Dotty accompanied Mary to the radiologist's office. When she came home, her usually perfectly coiffed hair lay limp. "You okay?" I asked. "How did things go?"

She shrugged. "Okay, I guess. But you know these doctors."

I smiled. Intimately, I thought.

"The radiologist wouldn't tell her anything. He said to call the pathologist in a few days and gave her his number. Mary looked devastated—not from the pain of the procedure, but from the uncertainty of not knowing. It's mind blowing."

"I know, but it takes that long to prepare the slides before the pathologist to read them."

"Could you expedite matters?"

"I could try, but they won't give me the results. I'm not her doctor or her relative."

Dotty cocked her head and lifted her eyebrows. "Please?"

"Since you put it that way, okay. But no promises."

She smiled. "At least Mary's guy was there. He's good looking, charming, and seemed supportive. But . . ."

"What?"

"I hope he doesn't bolt if the path report comes back cancer."

"I hope not."

The next day, I called to get the results. But since I didn't know the pathologist personally, apparently I had no standing with him, and he wouldn't give me a heads up. "Besides," he said. "I won't have the final result until tomorrow. Tell your friend to call the radiologist's office. They'll have my report by noon."

Sounds like the pathologist and radiologist were playing a game of football, punting back and forth without taking a stand.

I told Dotty what he had said, and by the pout on her face, and the way her eyes bored into mine, I could tell she wasn't happy. "If you were getting the results for me, you wouldn't have any trouble," she said."

"That's different."

"How so?"

"You're my wife. She's just an acquaintance. Don't be angry. I tried but just couldn't do it."

Dotty's eyes drove deeper. I put my hands in front of my face to deflect the daggers. She turned and walked down the hall. "If you say so."

I knew this animosity was a reflection of her angst over Mary. I chased her down the hall. "Why don't you take Mary to lunch tomorrow? You could be with her when she calls for the results."

Dotty turned, and her eyes boring into mine were not as penetrating. "Good idea. I think I will."

When she returned from lunch the next day, Dotty was ashen. "It's malignant. Now the shit starts all over again. It was bigger than her last one, so they'll probably want to be more aggressive. You know, another mastectomy and stronger chemotherapy." Her hand wandered to her breast. "I feel so bad for Mary."

I put my arms around Dotty. "I know, sweetheart. I'm sure you'll be supportive."

Through her tears, all she could manage was a nod.

Dotty had proved prophetic. The plan for Mary was another mastectomy and then harsh chemotherapy. On the day of Mary's surgery, Dotty and I sat in the surgical waiting room with Mary's good friend Donna—the one who had the benign breast biopsy. The two women were chatting away, while I immersed myself in the sports section, memorizing the statistics of the Miami Heat basketball players.

"Why Mary?" Donna said. "Why should she have it twice? She's been through so much."

Dotty shook her head. "I know, it just isn't fair. But then again, who says the world has to be fair? At least Mary has good friends and her guy. She'll get through it. By the way, where is he?"

Donna shook her head.

"Why are you shaking your head?" Dotty asked.

"That SOB who seemed so supportive, so understanding, up and bolted when she was diagnosed with the second cancer. He was crude enough to say, he wanted a wife who would be around for awhile."

Dotty put the back of her hand in front of her mouth and opened her eyes wide. "Men are such shits."

I cocked my head toward her.

Dotty smiled. "Of course, not you, sweetheart."

"Yeah sure."

We were interrupted by the surgeon who informed us that Mary's surgery went well. How could it have gone well, I thought? To have lost your second breast to cancer was not my idea of going well. Now the long road of chemotherapy begins again for her. I looked at Dotty and was grateful she wasn't in that position. I wondered if Dotty's breast cancer would always be an anvil on our backs—would always be a drag on our lives.

As we left the hospital, I put my arm around Dotty. "She's going to need all the support she can get. I'm sure you'll be there for her."

"You bet."

I hoped that over the ensuing months, her support for Mary would enable Dotty not to fixate on herself. But somehow, I doubted it, because I, too, had let fear creep into my life. Although I hoped it wouldn't happen, and acted with self assurance in front of Dotty, I dreaded that another blow would land on us.

Six months later, Mary had completed her chemotherapy, and was doing well. She was cancer free and was facing the future with hope. She told us that she wanted to live life to the fullest since she was well aware of how fleeting it could be. Dotty, on the other hand, became more withdrawn and fearful that a recurrence was around the bend, like a gunman waiting for a stagecoach in the Old West. This stymied our ability to make major life decisions, like moving to a condo on the beach or planning our dream trip to Australia and New Zealand. My brother had a similar reaction several years before, when he had been treated for prostate cancer. Although his prognosis was good, he planned for death, instead of embracing life. He talked about not wanting to be away for long periods, so he would be near his doctors. He bought a condominium Dotty and I owned in Manhattan, so his wife would have a home after he was gone—a home unencumbered by the vagaries of renting. He talked about end of life issues without regard to the joys of the present. I was dismayed that Dotty had taken a similar stance. My experience with patients parents who had developed cancer was that they had reactions similar to Mary's. They wanted to get everything out of life while they still had the strength. I realized though, that one size truly didn't fit all.

One evening, I was slouched in my father's lounge chair, reading a spy book by Robert Ludlam. Dotty, who was sprawled on the couch also reading, jumped up. Her hand was under her pajama top resting on her breast. "Paul, feel this."

She took my hand and ran it over the area she was feeling. I manipulated my fingertips over a soft, two to three inch, moveable mass. Just a cyst, I hoped. But the thought racing through my mind was here we go again. "It's probably just a cyst," I said. "You've had them before."

"This is different."

"How so?"

"No pain or tenderness."

That is disturbing, I thought. "Why don't we just get a mammogram and sonogram to check it out. Although, I'm sure it's nothing."

I could see my words were like daggers that dug deep. Dotty grabbed at her breast. "No, I can't believe this. Remember when Mary reminded me that having had cancer in one breast makes it more likely to develop it in the other? Well, in Mary's case, that's what happened. I know that's what's going to happen to me."

"No you don't. It feels like a cyst. Let's not panic until we check it out."

Dotty kept shaking her head, as tears flowed. I stood up, grasped her in my arms and we clung to each other.

Two days later we were in the radiologist's office having the tests. I was grateful, that since I had cared for his children, he worked us into his schedule without a three week wait. As we sat with him in the reading room watching him peruse her past and present X-rays, I trembled. "It looks like a fibroadenoma," he said. "But it wasn't there eight months ago. That is a little unusual." He turned to Dotty and tried to explain his findings in lay terms.

"It really just looks like a benign cyst, and therefore nothing to worry about. But . . ."

Dotty interrupted. "How do you know?"

"I was just about to say the only way to know for sure is to do a biopsy."

"Should we?"

"I really think that would be best."

I chimed in. "Could we get it scheduled as soon as possible?" I didn't want Dotty to sit around, since the fear of not knowing might be worse for her than the reality. "Is that okay, sweetheart?"

Her face was drawn and sullen, and she rubbed her eyes before answering. "I guess."

"How about tomorrow?" the radiologist said. "It's not like your first one that looked like cancer and I sent you directly to the surgeon. I really think it's going to be benign. If it is, they turn cancerous about as often as pigs fly."

I hoped he was clairvoyant, and this whole episode would be some fast forgotten blimp, but I was aware that whatever the outcome, this would not be. The radiologist explained the procedure, but I was sure from the blank look on Dotty's face, she had tuned him out.

The next day, after a sleepless night, Dotty and I sat in the radiologist's waiting room. I was doing what had become customary for me, flipping through magazines, trying to catch up on the news. To my annoyance, the magazines were three months old, and provided me with no new insights. I flung them back in the stand and turned to Dotty. "I wonder what's taking so long?"

"Me too."

"Maybe he's behind because he fit you in?"

"That makes no sense," Dotty said. "If that were the case, he wouldn't be behind until after I was done. Why don't you go ask?"

I started to get up, when Dotty's name was called. The assistant explained that the last biopsy was a difficult one and took a lot longer than expected. I hoped this wouldn't be the case with Dotty. We stood outside the procedure room while they cleaned up after the last patient. Then Dotty put on a gown and was placed on a table next to the ultrasound machine. It would be used to locate the exact spot of her tumor and eliminate any guesswork. I was allowed to sit in the corner to watch, hold Dotty's hand, and be supportive.

After five minutes, the radiologist came in, checked the equipment and walked over to Dotty. "Are you ready?"

Her head wobbled back and forth like a bobble head doll. "I guess I'm as ready as I'll ever be."

"Okay, let's get started."

He filled up a syringe with topical anaesthetic and jabbed Dotty in the breast above the tumor, pushing the clear fluid into the surrounding tissue.

"Ow, that hurts." Dotty said.

He rubbed her breast to ensure equal distribution of the liquid. "Now you won't feel anything else. When I stick you with the needle to get the biopsy, you won't have any pain."

I didn't know about Dotty, but I sure was having pain. My stomach felt like it was being devoured by termites gobbling wood, and my hand ached where Dotty had squeezed so hard as the needle entered her breast. I echoed the radiologist's words. "You won't feel anything else."

The radiologist ran the ultrasound wand over her breast until the tumor appeared on the screen. He took the biopsy needle, punctured Dotty's skin and probed for the mass. Every time the tip of the needle touched the mass it jumped away, almost as if it was autonomous and didn't want to be violated. I felt like jumping away too—right out of the room. I'm sure Dotty had the same feeling too, only magnified many times.

At last the mass yielded and allowed the needle to penetrate. "Got you," the radiologist said. He manipulated the instrument, took some samples, and withdrew the needle. "I'm going to send the specimen to Hollywood Medical Center. They have a great pathologist there." He turned to me. "I'll give you his name and number. The results should be ready tomorrow morning. Call him."

Then he focused his attention on Dotty. "I'm pretty sure it's going to be fine. We'll know tomorrow. When you get home put some ice on the area where we did the biopsy in order to keep the swelling down. You shouldn't have much pain, but if you experience any take Tylenol."

He hurriedly left the room, as Dotty dressed. Probably trying to catch up to his schedule, I thought. "Are you okay?" I asked.

"As good as I can be."

"Good. Let's go home and have a glass of wine so we can drink to a happy ending tomorrow."

She nodded and pointed to the sky. "From your mouth to His ears."

"Maybe it's Her ears," I said again. I smiled.

Dotty returned my smile.

After a restless night, and a gulped down breakfast, I called the pathologist. I explained who I was and what I was calling about, but to my chagrin I had called too soon. The results wouldn't be ready for a few hours. He would call.

When I told Dotty, she banged her fist into her forehead. "Damn!"

About an hour later, when the phone rang, I grabbed the receiver. My heart was pounding. It was my son. I told him we'd call as soon as we had the results. Just before noon, the ringing of the phone interrupted my melancholy mood.

"I just finished," the pathologist said.

"So tell me."

"It's a benign fibroadenoma," he said. "No trace of malignancy."

I exhaled a chestful of air, thanked the pathologist, and gave Dotty the thumbs up sign. "It's over," I said. "Everything is benign."

She smiled and flung her arms around me. We lingered for a few minutes before separating. "I'm going to the bedroom to call everyone. I can't wait to tell them the news."

I lay down on the couch to watch test patterns on TV, to drained to do anything else. About an hour later, Dotty pushed me. "Wake up lazy bones. I'm going to let you take me out to lunch."

"My pleasure."

As we were getting ready, Dotty plopped down on the bed to put her shoes on. "Oh, by the way, Mary says hello. She and her friend Donna are taking a cruise around Australia and New Zealand. She asked if we'd like to go along. I told her no, that I was emotionally drained and couldn't commit to doing it right now. But maybe you and I will do it another time."

I nodded, as I stared at the lithograph on our wall. It was an artistic rendition of a saying by Hillel the Elder of Babylon. I read the last line of the saying over and over. "And if not now when? And if not now when?"

Chapter Eighteen

–Deja Vu–Biopsy Two

Seven years had passed. Mary, like Dotty, was still in remission. She had carried out her pledge to live life to its fullest, traveling all over the world, seizing business opportunities, and even meeting a new man with whom she was living. Dotty on the other hand, lived life like she was a football waiting to be kicked for a field goal that would go wide right. She withdrew into a shell and became somewhat forgetful. Toward the end of that time though, I had hopes that things would change. We put a down payment on our dream condominium, which was being constructed on Hollywood Beach. Dotty showed some excitement because it was exactly what we wanted, spacious, overlooking the ocean to the east and a park to the north, close to our old haunts, and near our children and grandchildren. Dotty was even feeling well enough to talk about going to Australia and New Zealand. She even joked, she would go in a heartbeat if she could magically be transported there.

One day, I was lounging on the patio, reading a pediatric journal, while sucking on a popsicle. Dotty came out carrying the portable phone. "Dana's on the phone," she said.

From the way Dotty said it, and from the frown on her face, I sensed trouble. I wondered what my cousin wanted? "What's the matter?" I mouthed.

"Something about a mammogram irregularity," Dotty said. "She wants to talk to you."

Here we go again, I thought. Please let it be nothing. I grabbed the phone. "Hi Dana, how are you?"

"Cuz, I'm freaked out of my mind"

"What's the matter?"

"I had my mammogram."

"I know. You said it was fine."

"That's what the technician said. But today the secretary called and told me there was an irregularity on the mammogram and they wanted me to come back for another mammogram and sonogram."

I sat up in the lounger. "What kind of irregularity?"

"That's what I asked, but the secretary didn't know. All she said was that most of the recalls turn out to be nothing, and I shouldn't worry."

I thought to myself, sure don't worry. Tell a woman there's something wrong with her mammogram and expect her to feel no concern. Right!

"The first appointment they had was for three weeks from now. Could you please find out what the hell they found. If I really need to have these tests done, could we get them sooner?"

I stood up and walked toward my hospital directory that had the phone numbers of all the departments at Memorial Hospital. Dana's tests were done in the radiology department there. "I'll try getting through right now, and call you as soon as I hear anything."

When I got off the phone with Dana, I told Dotty what she had said. Her reaction was expected. She put the back of her hand to her mouth. "Please God, let it be nothing."

I put my arm around Dotty and squeezed. "Now, let me call the radiologist and find out what's going on."

When my call was answered, a recorded sing-song went through a potpourri of options. This time I was wiser. I jabbed O to get the operator and asked for the radiology reading room. After identifying myself, the radiologist I reached was very accommodating. He looked up Dana's report and reviewed her X-rays, as I held on. When he got back on the line, I felt my body stiffen. "She has what looks like three small micro-calcifications," he said. "However, they might be artifacts. Probably nothing, but we should check it out."

"Will a repeat mammogram and sonogram be absolutely definitive?" I asked.

"There are no absolutes in medicine. You know that. But if the calcifications aren't there on a repeat study, then we can stop, and be pretty sure."

I realized he meant that if they were still there, Dana would need a biopsy, and that this was, in all likelihood, what would happen. The fact that the radiologist thought that everything would prove benign gave me some relief, but until we knew definitively, my angst would rise to new heights, as would Dotty's and Dana's. I decided not to tell my cousin about the possibility of a biopsy until it was definitely decided that this was the route to take. Besides, that proclamation should come from her primary care physician or her radiologist. I was able to accomplish scheduling Dana's tests for the following week.

I called Dana to give her the information. "It's going to be okay, isn't it?" she asked.

"I'm pretty sure. Let's get the tests and go from there."

"What do you mean. Go where?" she asked.

She was too smart for me. She had sensed from my language and the tone of my voice that I might be holding back something. "You might need a biopsy. The radiologist is pretty sure it's nothing. Wait till you have the tests. If they confirm the calcifications, you might want to have a biopsy even though it's not likely to show anything bad. You know Dotty had one seven or eight years ago and everything was fine. It will be the same for you."

Despite my reassurances, I could sense my cousin's anxiety level escalating, and the truth be told, so was mine. The fact that everything pointed to a benign outcome, didn't relieve my tension. Sensitized by Dotty having had breast cancer, whenever anything in a breast was mentioned, I cringed. I realized my feelings had to be magnified in my cousin and would reach humongous proportions when I told Dotty what I had learned.

My estimation of Dotty's reaction was right on the mark. She called Dana, who she adored, stifling tears, while trying to be reassuring. After they hung up, a torrent was released from Dotty's eyes. Dotty buried her face in her hands, as the tears kept coming. "Why does this keep happening?" she asked.

"The last time you were okay, and I'm sure it will be this time," I said. I put my arm around Dotty. "You can't fall apart. We need to be supportive."

She nodded. "I know I'll be okay. I just hope Dana is too."

The next week, Dana went for her tests. When she returned, she called me. "How did you make out?" I asked.

"I don't know. They wouldn't tell me anything. Could you call and get the results?"

"You bet. I'll call you as soon as I get some information."

I called the radiologist. I was grateful he had given me his private number. I didn't have to deal with the sing-song recorded messages or the myriad of options they offered. "I just finished looking at the films," he said. "Those areas that I saw weren't artifacts, but definitely micro-calcifications. Although everything looks benign, I really think she should have a biopsy."

Here we go again, I thought. If there's any chance of it being malignant, Dana had the same choice Dotty did—none. "Will you do me a favor? Will you call my cousin and tell her what you just told me?"

When he said he would, I thanked him, and sat down in my blue recliner—the one that matched my mood. I contemplated whether I should call Dana right away. I didn't want to be the bearer of bad tidings. Although she leaned on me for medical advice, I wasn't her doctor. It was one thing to expedite matters, but another to make medical decisions. The way this thing had been handled so far was a nightmare. Having a secretary call to tell Dana there was an irregularity on the X-ray that warranted further tests had heightened her anxiety. I wanted to mollify it, not magnify it.

Before deciding whether to call, the phone rang. "Cuz, the radiologist called."

"I know. I just spoke to him."

"Then you know, he wants to do a biopsy."

My head bobbled up and down. "I know."

"What do you think?"

I feared discussing this. That's why I had procrastinated calling her. But I felt I was boxed in and had no choice. "It's not my decision, but let's look at this rationally. The biopsy probably will be benign, which means you will have undergone a needless, somewhat painful procedure. That's the downside. The upside is you'll know for sure, which will take a weight off your shoulders. On the rare chance that it is cancer, it will have been caught early, and can easily be dealt with." I tried to leave the decision to Dana, but realized that what I had said would push her to have the biopsy. Then again, she was smarter than me, and I was sure she'd figure that out for herself.

"What choice do I have?" she said. "I'll call and make an appointment."

"Dotty and I want to be there. If you have any trouble scheduling it call me."

Fifteen minutes later, Dana called back. "The first appointment is in five weeks. I'll go crazy if I have to sit around and think about this for so long."

"Let me call, and see what I can do."

I called the interventional radiology department, and was grateful the scheduling clerk's children had been patients of mine. She fit Dana into the schedule for the following week. I knew this service wasn't an option open to most patients, but I didn't feel guilty. I had given a lot of blood and sweat to the hospital, and felt I was entitled to this and other courtesies. Still, I was sorry for those who didn't have this advantage, and would have to agonize while enduring a long wait to have their tests, in order to find out whether or not they had breast cancer. I knew though, that people at all walks of life, availed themselves of whatever edge they could latch onto.

I called Dana to tell her the news. Through the phone line, I could hear her exhale. "Thanks, Cuz."

The following week, Dotty and I sat in the Women's Breast Center with Dana. While she filled out forms, I flipped through outdated magazines. I relished reliving the Miami Heat's championship from two years before as detailed in an old Sports Illustrated. Dotty tried to comfort Dana, but was ineffectual because she had trouble stifling her own emotions. After a half hour, when Dana still hadn't been called, Dotty turned to me. "Maybe you could do something?" she said.

I nodded, walked across the room, and followed an assistant who was escorting another patient back to the treatment area. At the desk, I interrupted a nurse who was scribbling on a chart. When she looked at me, she smiled. "Dr. Winick?" she asked.

I nodded, staring at the blond haired, blue eyed woman, hoping to recognize her.

"Debbie Weiss," she said. "You knew me as Debbie Hauser before I was married."

Of course I knew her. I had cared for her and her siblings for years. "Debbie, how are you? How's the family?"

"Everyone's good."

After catching up on family happenings, I told her we had been waiting a long time, and asked if there was anything she could do to expedite matters.

"Dana's your cousin?"

I nodded. "Always has been."

"Does she have a child who went to Nova High?"

"She sure does."

"We were classmates. I'll do my best to get your cousin back as soon as possible."

I went back and told everyone what had transpired. "I remember Debbie," Dana said. "Very pretty, good athlete, definitely a sweetheart."

Five minutes later, Dana was called. Maybe Debbie had something to do with that, or it was just Dana's turn. Dotty and I sat in the waiting room doing just that, waiting and waiting. I paced the room a number of times out of nervousness and also to stretch my recently replaced hips. Just as I was about to inquire what was going on, Debbie came out.

"What's taking so long?" I asked.

"We haven't started yet. Dana's blood pressure soared to 160 over 105. If it doesn't come down with relaxation they're going to cancel the procedure. I'll keep you informed."

Poor Dana, I thought. She must be scared out of her mind. How do they expect her to relax with all this hanging over her head. If they don't do the procedure her angst will just escalate to the next level, as would Dotty's and mine.

A half hour later, Debbie came out again. "Her pressure's down to 145 over 95. They're about to start."

I smiled. "Thank you," I said.

We sat down to continue our vigil, engrossed in our own thoughts. I looked at my watch and saw an hour had gone by. What could be taking so long? I shifted my weight in the chair, and was about to lift myself up in order to pace the floors again, when Dana came bounding out. "How did it go?" I asked.

"The biopsy was nothing. A little discomfort, that's all. All that waiting, though, made me a nervous wreck. I've never had a blood pressure so high."

I kissed her cheeks. "You're right, probably just nerves. It's called white coat hypertension."

"Should I do anything about it?"

"Let your internist know and have your pressure checked frequently. Stress can do it, but it should return to normal now." What if the biopsy is positive, I thought? What then?

Dana nodded. "They said the results would take from a few days to a week. Could you see if you could get them sooner?"

"You bet. I'll call tomorrow."

I didn't wait that long. When I got home, I called the pathologist who would be reading the biopsy, and identified myself. He said to call the next day around noon, and he'd have the results for me.

At precisely noon, I called the pathologist. "Good news," he said. "All the slides are benign. However, I didn't get any cuts through the micro-calcifications, so I'll have to make some finer slices in order to sample that area. They won't be ready until tomorrow." More anxiety, I thought. But at least, so far so good.

I called Dana to tell her. "We won't know for sure until he explores that area," she said. "Isn't that so?"

"I guess that's true, but he sampled the majority of the specimen, and it's okay,"

Through the phone, I heard deep breathing. "Damn," she said. "I wish we knew for sure."

"I'll call tomorrow as soon as I know anything."

The next day, when I reached the pathologist, it was deja vu. "This batch of slides didn't get the calcifications either," he said. "I'm going to make one more attempt. Call tomorrow."

I wondered if it was the elusiveness of the calcifications and their infinitesimal size that was causing the difficulty, or his incompetence. I knew of his impeccable reputation, so for now I concluded it was the former.

"This is ridiculous," Dotty said. "We could have gone to China and back for as long as this is taking. But at least there's no bad news yet. Let me call Dana and tell her."

I nodded. I was grateful not to have to listen to my cousin's cracking voice. It was difficult for me to provide comfort as my increasing agitation was causing my arms to feel like an orange being squeezed. I was glad that no one had to take my blood pressure. "Tell Dana, I'll call tomorrow."

When Dotty got off the phone, she told me Dana had cried. "Tell me it's going to be okay. Please tell me."

"I think so, but . . ." I shrugged.

The next day I called the pathologist, and tapped the phone against my temple, as I waited for him to get on the line. "Good news," he said. "We got the calcifications, and everything surrounding them is benign. I'm going to sign the biopsy out as benign fibroadenoma with micro-calcifications."

I exhaled, and thanked him. I told Dotty, who smiled, as I dialed Dana's number.

"Cuz, I really appreciate everything you did, and I'm relieved everything's okay. Let's just hope it stays that way."

"You bet, and Dotty and I owe you a dinner to celebrate. We'll set up a time."

When I got off the phone, I knew this nightmare would never end. It had been six or seven years since Dotty's biopsy, before the next sword had fallen. I no longer wondered if it would happen again. I only wondered when.

Chapter Nineteen

–Barbara

Three weeks after Dana's negative biopsy, we were finishing dinner when the phone rang. It was Murray, the husband of another cousin. "I can't wake Barbara!" he screamed. "What should I do?"

"Call 911. I'm on my way. I'll probably beat them there."

As I rushed out the door, Dotty yelled. "I hope she's okay. She's such a nice person and I know how special she is to you."

Barbara was not only my cousin and friend, but my sports mentor. I attributed part of my love for baseball to her. She was nine years older than I was, and a rabid Dodger fan, which I then emulated. We both felt that if we bled it would be Dodger blue. In later years, she was my buddy at Miami Heat basketball games. We would sit on a railroad transformer outside, the old Miami Arena, eating sausage dogs and other junk food, before going to the game. We would discuss life, and family. She was the quintessential grandmother, not because of filial duty, but because her grandchildren always leaned on her for advice and support. I hoped I could emulate her with my grandchildren. I missed this time together for the past two years, because Barbara was too sick and in too much pain to attend any basketball games. Years of hard to control asthma often left her struggling to breathe if she had to walk from the parking lot to the arena and then up the stairs. Her extreme back pain, exacerbated by her long use of cortisone to control her asthma, was debilitating and made walking and sitting for prolonged periods difficult.

As I pulled into the apartment complex, I saw the paramedics hadn't yet arrived yet. I hoped Barbara would be okay. Inside, I stared at my cousin. She was lying in bed without moving. Her breathing was shallow, and her normally bronze complexion had a ghostlike pallor. I knew she had been taking a blood thinner for heart fibrillations and wondered if she had a stroke with bleeding into the brain like my mother did—like what I worried about when Dotty was receiving chemotherapy and her clotting factors were low. I also wondered if she had taken an overdose of pain killers, either deliberate or otherwise. That too would explain what I was observing,

When the paramedics arrived, they harbored the same thoughts as the ones I was having. After ascertaining that Barbara was stable, they put her in the ambulance and rushed her to Hollywood Memorial Hospital, where I had practiced for years. Murray and I followed by car. When we arrived at the emergency room, Barbara was more alert, and was being rushed into X-ray for a CAT scan of the brain. The study proved negative, there was no evidence of a stroke. She was admitted to the ward for a complete evaluation. I hoped she hadn't taken an overdose, and they would find a simple, easily treatable, explanation for her symptoms. I wanted more time with my cousin.

By the time I reached the ward, Barbara was alert enough to talk. She had no recollection of what had happened. Her doctor arrived, examined her, and also was at a loss to explain Barbara's symptoms. He ordered a bunch of tests including a chest X-ray, an MRI scan of her brain, a number of blood tests, and a urine toxicology screen to see if she had taken an overdose of pain killers. When he left, I leaned over and kissed Barbara on the forehead. "It's getting past my bedtime, Cuz. Dotty and I will see you tomorrow."

When I came home Dotty grilled me as to the cause of Barbara's illness. I shrugged. "Let's wait till we get the test results back."

"Could she have cancer?"

"What makes you ask that?"

"Oh, I don't know. I guess it's the first thing I think about these days."

"You're fine and hopefully Barbara will be too." I put my arm around Dotty and squeezed. "Let's get some rest."

The next day when we went to visit Barbara, I excused myself to talk to her doctor who was standing at the nurses' station. He told me that her blood work was normal, as was her MRI scan. She had narcotic pain killers in her urine, but not enough to have caused her symptoms. Then, he hesitated and cleared his throat before continuing. "However, the chest x-ray showed a significant mass on her left lung."

"Could it be an infection?"

"I doubt it. It looks more like a cancer. We'll have to biopsy it to find out."

"What kind?"

He shrugged. "Probably lung, but maybe a lymphoma."

"Damn!" I said.

I hoped it was a lymphoma because it had a better prognosis. I knew Dotty wasn't clairvoyant and was just projecting her own fears when she asked if Barbara could have cancer. Fears that would be magnified when Dotty found out. I was sure that I would be in for dealing with Dotty's heightened insecurities, while trying to help my cousin navigate through her upcoming ordeal.

After the doctor told Barbara, Dotty and I stayed for support. Dotty's complexion was pale, but Barbara took the news in stride. "I'm not going to do anything," she said. "I know the terrible prognosis with lung cancer. I'm in enough pain already, and don't need to be poked and prodded anymore. What will be will be."

"You have to have the biopsy," I said. "There's a small chance that it's not cancer, and if it is, maybe it's a lymphoma, which is easily treatable. You haven't smoked in years, making lung cancer less likely."

Barbara stared at me, and shook her head. I guessed that what I said about her smoking wasn't quite true. Had she been a closet smoker without my knowledge? Even so, I continued nagging her about the lung biopsy until she finally agreed to the procedure.

That night, Dotty became weepy eyed and non-communicative. I tried to be reassuring, but my words were landing on deaf ears. I knew Dotty was upset about Barbara who she dearly loved, but I also sensed she was contemplating her own mortality. This was a scenario I was used to whenever we heard about a friend or acquaintance who had developed cancer, not to mention the intensity of her feelings when a relative was involved. All I could do was hover and remain close, hoping the fear would abate. I knew it would never fully dissipate.

The next day, we arrived as they were wheeling Barbara on a stretcher, to take her for the biopsy. "I really don't want to do this," she said.

"It will be okay."

After she was gone, I spoke to Murray. "What's the matter with Barbara? She doesn't seem to have any zest for life."

"I think you're right. She's been in a lot of pain with her back, and her asthma is out of control. At times, she has trouble breathing."

"Do you think she might take an overdose of pain killers?"

He shrugged. "Maybe."

If this were the case, was I making things worse by insisting she have all these invasive tests—a lung biopsy, tests such as a spinal tap to stage whatever cancer she had, and then either surgery, chemotherapy or both. I wondered if Dotty had harbored any of these thoughts when she was diagnosed with breast cancer. I remembered, she had become withdrawn and somewhat non-communicative. I hoped it was because of fear of the unknown and the ordeal ahead, and not because she had thoughts of taking an overdose. This was the same hope I had for my cousin in her present situation. If not, I feared I was making the situation worse. Despite this thought, I knew that with my medical background, and my love for Barbara, I would push her to do anything possible so that we could have more time together.

The surgeon popped his head into the waiting room where we sat deep in our own thoughts. "She did fine," he said. "It's definitely a cancer, but grossly, it doesn't look like the typical lung cancer. We'll know more tomorrow, when the pathologist looks at the slides."

How could she have done fine, I thought? I wanted to scream, she has cancer.

That night, I spoke on the phone to Barbara's two children, one in Nashville, the other in New York. I explained to them the difference between lung cancer and lymphoma—how lymphoma had a better prognosis and in all likelihood would only require chemotherapy. Lung cancer, on the other hand, was a much more aggressive tumor and would require surgery, chemotherapy and perhaps radiation. I told them that we'd speak again as soon as we had the pathologist's results, and a course of therapy had been decided on.

The next day, we got the news that Barbara had a large cell follicular lymphoma, a kind readily responsive to chemotherapy. I expected Barbara to feel the same relief I felt, but all she did was shrug. How could either of us feel relief given that she still had a diagnosis of cancer, and was facing a long ordeal?

"What now?" she asked.

"We'll make an appointment with an oncologist. He'll probably want to run some tests to stage the cancer, before treating you."

"What kind of tests?"

"I don't know. Maybe a bone marrow exam or a spinal tap. Let's wait and see what he says." Barbara, who had been a medical assistant, knew exactly what I was talking about.

"Why can't they just leave me alone."

I tried to be upbeat. "Barbara, the kind of tumor you have is very amenable to treatment. You should do whatever it takes."

She shrugged.

I wondered again if I was doing the right thing. Was I projecting my own feelings on to my cousin, and was not being sensitive to hers? After all, her medical fate should be her decision. I leaned over and kissed her forehead.

Several days after Barbara left the hospital, we went to see the oncologist who her primary care physician recommended. It was Dr. Wayling, the same oncologist that had frightened Dotty and caused her to tune him out. In this case, he was much more empathetic, and kept trying to reassure my cousin that she had a cancer that was very amenable to treatment. He outlined the chemotherapy she would need and what side effect she might experience.

"Before we start the chemotherapy," he said. "We'll need to do certain tests to properly stage the cancer. That way we'll know the proper drugs to use, and the dose and length of treatment."

"What tests?" Barbara asked.

"We'll have to do a bone marrow exam, a spinal tap, and probably an MRI of the abdomen. You'll also need to have a port—that is, we'll need to thread a catheter into a vein and leave it in place. That way, we'll have easy access when we start therapy. Do you understand?"

Barbara shook her head. "I do, but I don't want any of this." She looked at me. "Why do I have to go through the torture of tests and treatment? I'm in enough pain already."

"So you can have more time with your husband, children and grandchildren—more time with me."

"When Dr. Wayling stepped out of the room, I put my arm around Barbara. "Why don't we get another opinion down at the university. Maybe, they'll want to get less tests and give you milder chemotherapy."

She shook her head.

In my heart, I knew what Dr. Wayling had outlined was proper procedure, but I wasn't completely sure. Was I still being pushy because of the way I felt and wasn't taking her feelings into account? After all, hadn't I said to Dotty on a number of occasions, it was my job to support her decisions, not make them for her. "I'm sure Dr. Wayling would make all the arrangements for the consult and would be willing to provide you whatever care the people at the university deemed necessary," I said.

Barbara stared at me for what seemed like an eternity. I was sure she was mulling over what I had said. Finally, she nodded.

When Dr. Wayling returned, he agreed to the plan I had laid out. He was kind enough to make an appointment for Barbara for the following week. I told Barbara and Murray that I would pick up all the tests results, and the slides from her cancer, and bring them with me when I drove them down to Barbara's appointment.

For the first time in days, my cousin's lips elevated, trying to form a smile. I put my arm around her and kissed her forehead. I'll see you next week, and Dotty and I will call every day to see how you're doing."

Barbara's smile broadened. "Thank you," she said.

That night, I held Dotty in my arms as I told her about Barbara. She looked up at me through mascara smudged eyes. "Why has cancer afflicted our family so hard?" I guessed she was thinking about her own mortality, as well as Barbara's.

"Cancer affects a lot of families. It certainly hasn't singled ours out. The good news is that Barbara has a readily treatable form of cancer. Even better than yours, and look how well you've done."

"So far," she said. "So far."

With that comment, I wondered if Dotty would ever stop worrying? Would her mind be freed to enjoy life the way she did before breast cancer crept into our lives?

We stood clinging to each other, swaying back and forth. "Let's go out to dinner." I said.

She nodded.

The next week, I picked Barbara and Murray up for the drive down to the University. This was a drive I had grown accustomed to because of all the volunteer teaching I had done in the Pediatric Department through the years. Barbara looked sallow and sat hunched over in the front seat. Murray had warned me that she wasn't doing well. "What's the matter?" I asked.

My asthma has flared up and I can't sleep. The excruciating pains in my back don't help either."

"Maybe your breathing problem and pains are related to your cancer, and you'll get relief after your treatment."

"Yeah, sure. Tell me another story."

Barbara could always see through me. She realized I was grasping at straws. I think I fooled myself more than I fooled her. Maybe I needed to get out of doctor mode and into loving cousin mode.

When we arrived for her appointment, I dropped Barbara and Murray in front of the clinic, and drove to the parking garage, where I found a spot on the sixth floor. By the time I joined them, they had completed the paperwork and were being ushered into an examining room. How efficient, I thought. We waited only a few minutes, when a young man, clad in a white coat, entered and introduced himself as Dr. Marks' fellow. Barbara looked at him quizzically. The fellow must have sensed what she was thinking. "Dr. Marks will be with you in a little while," he said. "After I've taken a complete history and done a thorough physical exam. Okay?"

Barbara nodded.

He helped Barbara onto the examining table. This wasn't an easy task, as Barbara grimaced as she maneuvered herself onto the table. After a half hour of poking her and asking questions, he finished. "I'll get Dr. Marks," he said.

By the time they returned fifteen minutes later, Barbara was hunched over, grabbing her back, and was wheezing. Dr. Marks, picked up the record, asked a few questions, and felt her neck and abdomen. After listening to her chest, he smiled. "I think the treatment for your lymphoma might help the wheezing. I agree with everything Dr. Wayling told you. The lymphoma you have is a large cell follicular non-Hodgkin's lymphoma. It has an excellent prognosis. The chemotherapy he outlined to you is the same protocol we're using down here. However, we might want to change it depending on the results of a few more tests that I'm going to recommend.

"What tests?" Barbara asked.

"A bone marrow and spinal fluid exam, to make sure the central nervous system and the blood stream aren't involved. We'll also have to do an MRI of your abdomen to make sure there's no involvement of those nodes. When those tests are done, you'll need to have a port placed to allow easy access to a vein when you have your chemotherapy."

Barbara opened her mouth to talk, but didn't say anything. She just shook her head.

"Do you have any questions?" Dr. Marks asked.

Barbara only shook her head harder.

On the way home, Barbara asked, "Why can't they just leave me alone? I don't want to go through any of this."

"Because you have grandchildren's weddings to go to and we have ball games to watch together," I said.

She shrugged. "If you say so."

Even if she was doing this for me, I believed her outcome would justify my pushing her into accepting treatment. If things didn't work out, I knew I'd feel awful for adding to her suffering. I hoped the torrential rain we were driving into was not a bad omen.

The following week, Barbara was admitted to the hospital for the tests and to have a port placed. When I came to visit, she smiled. "I think they're trying to kill me." She rubbed her back and hip where they had done the spinal tap and bone marrow exam. "If my back hurt before, it's ten times worse now."

"I know, but that too will pass."

She opened her mouth to speak, but was interrupted when Dr. Wayling came into the room. After the usual pleasantries, "All your tests are normal" he said. "You can start the chemotherapy. that we outlined, next week."

"Isn't that great," I said.

"You're kidding. If they didn't kill me today, they can poison me next week."

I had never known Barbara to be sarcastic. Again, the thought occurred to me, that she was going through this whole ordeal just to please me. I hoped not, but even if she was, I still felt the ends, a healthy Barbara, justified the means. I realized though, that Barbara had no such feelings.

The following week, we took Barbara for her chemotherapy. The site of women wearing scarves around their heads brought back bad memories for me—memories of Dotty lying in one of the recumbent chairs, with chemotherapeutic drugs being pumped into her body. I hoped Barbara's outcome would be as good as Dotty's had been so far.

Barbara sat in the chair while a nurse accessed her port. A deepening frown accentuated the morose look permanently plastered on her face. I noticed one of my patient's mother in another chair, and excused myself to say hello.

"Hi Susan," I said. "How are you?"

She looked at the fluid dripping from the IV bag. "How should I be?"

She told me that like Barbara, she had a lymphoma, and this was her next to last treatment. She pointed to Barbara. "Is that your wife?"

"No, my cousin."

"She looks so sad. I was that way at the beginning, but it looks like I'm going to be okay."

"Good for you."

She smiled. "Tell your cousin that the people here are really nice and will make things as easy for her as they can. They have been a real comfort to me."

I thanked her and asked her to send my regards to her family. I told Barbara what Susan had said, but all she could do was shrug. "Good for her," she said.

When all the drugs had coursed through her veins, Barbara was so sleepy that it was hard to arouse her to go home. "It's all over," I said.

She looked at me through droopy eyes, and nodded. "Yes it is."

That evening, Dotty asked me if Barbara was going to be okay. "I don't know. I have my doubts."

Dotty's eyes filled with tears. "Barbara's situation is entirely different from yours. You're doing fine, and I'm sure you'll continue that way."

"I know, but . . ."

"No buts!"

She nodded. "Poor Barbara."

We were so exhausted that we went to bed right after dinner. When the phone rang at 7:00 the next morning, I fumbled for the receiver, looked at caller ID, and saw it was Murray. This can't be good, I thought.

Murray's voice was barely audible, "Barbara's dead," he said. "When I woke up this morning, she was ashen and wasn't breathing. The paramedics have already been here. Do you think she could have taken something?"

"I don't know. What difference does it make?" I started to tremble because I felt guilty for having put my cousin through the ordeal, if this was the way it was going to end. I would miss her. I realized, no matter the cause of her death, I wouldn't love her any less. I hoped again, Dotty hadn't harbored any thoughts of ending her own life, and wouldn't if she had a recurrence of the breast cancer. I also knew though, that if she did, I wouldn't love Dotty any less.

Chapter Twenty

–Recalling

The many cliches I had heard and spouted throughout the years never rang true—it's deja vu, it's God's will, what is meant to be will be, lightning never strikes twice in the same place. However, in this instance, it seemed that some, or all of the platitudes, might be accurate. It had been almost nine years since Dotty had her mastectomy for breast cancer, seven years since a biopsy of the mass in her opposite breast proved benign, and six or seven months since Dana's biopsy and Barbara's death. We had cancelled Dotty's dream trip to the Lands Down Under when her cancer was diagnosed. Although we had done some traveling, we had postponed major trips and some fun life decisions until now because Dotty had been too nervous to travel. We had purchased our dream condominium on Hollywood beach, and were about to close on it in the next few weeks. We were looking forward to retired tranquility, watching waves undulate across the shoreline, when our lives were hit by a potential tsunami. Was it God's will that anytime we planned life altering happenings a ton of bricks would fall? Was it deja vu? Were the cliches coming true?

Several days before her semiannual visit to her breast surgeon, and just six months after Barbara's death, Dotty became non-communicative. Fear that always hovered, gripped tighter as her appointment neared. When she returned from seeing him, her normal dark complexion had a slight pallor.

"How did you make out?" I asked

"Okay, I guess."

"What do you mean, okay, I guess?"

"Well, after the usual interminable wait, he examined my breast, felt the benign lump, then acted as if he didn't know about it. He flipped through the chart and said that the mass had gotten bigger on ultrasound. I told him I knew, and the radiologist said it was nothing to worry about. I mentioned I had a biopsy six or seven years ago. 'You did?' he said. 'I don't have a report. Let me call the radiologist's office and have it faxed over.'"

Dotty swallowed the spittle forming at the corners of her mouth. "When he left, I sat on the hard table and shivered, both with fright and because the air conditioning was blowing under the paper gown covering my chest."

I put my arms around Dotty and kissed her forehead.

"When he came back," Dotty said. "He was holding a piece of paper. 'You're right,' he said. 'Everything is okay. We'll see you in six months.'"

"That's terrific," I said. "Why don't we have a glass of wine to celebrate?"

"Good idea. I'm just beginning to calm down."

I poured us each a glass of merlot and held up my glass. "A toast—to new beginnings, to our new apartment, to life, L'Chaim." We clinked glasses.

The next morning while Dotty was out running errands, I completed a set of rehabilitation exercises designed to strengthen my two recently replaced hips. When finished, I mounted my stationary bike trying to work my way back to riding the twenty plus miles per day that I had done before my surgeries. When the phone rang, I reached over to answer while continuing to pedal. When I realized it was Dotty's breast surgeon, my legs stopped churning. After I told him Dotty wasn't home, he confided why he had called. He thought things over, and since Dotty's benign tumor had gotten larger he was concerned that malignant cells might be lurking within the confines of the mass. He thought it best that it be removed.

"What about if we did another biopsy?" I asked.

"You wouldn't be sampling all of it," he said. "And when we're done, we still wouldn't be sure."

"But the radiologist said that benign fibroadenomas turn into malignant cancer as often as pigs fly."

"Not my experience."

I stammered into the phone. "You're freaking me out."

"Probably will turn out to be nothing," he said. "But we should take it out."

"You need to talk to Dotty. It's not my place to tell her. She'll be in this afternoon."

After he said he'd call back, I mumbled a cursory goodbye, replaced the phone, gripped the handle bars, and leaning forward, I banged my head against the bike's frame. I dismounted, ran into the kitchen to look up a number, and cancelled my appointment for that afternoon. I wanted to be around, when the surgeon called back, to provide whatever comfort I could. I hoped Dotty wouldn't sense from my demeanor that something was awry.

Before she came home, I called two colleagues. One, another surgeon, said by all means take it out. Dotty, having had breast cancer once, was at increased risk for developing a second one, and occasionally fibroadenomas do turn malignant. The other, a radiologist, said there was no need to do anything, that fibroadenomas turn malignant as often as new cancers develop in the breast. Although in my heart, I felt the surgeon was making much ado about nothing, or at least that's what I wanted to believe, the seeds had been sown. I was sure Dotty would opt for the surgery. What choice did she have? The consequences of not removing the lump were too dire.

As I waited for her to come home, I hoped the right hyperbole would be correct—not deja vu, but lightning doesn't strike twice in the same place.

That afternoon, I tried to balance hovering with aloofness, not an easy task. When the phone rang, I sprang from my chair in the family room, where I was writing, and raced to the bedroom hallway where I lurked outside our door. Dotty, who was reading, answered the phone while I strained to hear. "I'd be happy to make the same contribution as last year," she said. "The Police Benevolent Association is a very worthy cause."

I tiptoed back to the family room. This was a round-trip I made four more times before supper, listening to Dotty answer calls from two friends and our son and daughter, but none from her breast surgeon. Why didn't he call back? Had he forgotten? Had he changed his mind? Did an emergency come up and he'd call the next day? I couldn't tell Dotty, that was his place. I didn't want her to know that I had talked to the surgeon. The decision should be hers.

The next day was a replay of the preceding one. I lingered close by when there was a call Dotty answered, but none were from her surgeon. The following day, Friday, when the scene repeated itself again, I was at a loss about to what to do, agitation having replaced rational thinking. I flipped pages in a book without absorbing a word. I wandered from room to room ending up in the kitchen where I stared blankly at our calendar. I remained transfixed with my mind swirling. Then I noticed Dotty had an appointment the following Tuesday to see her oncologist, Dr. Orgel. Maybe I could shift the decision-making burden over to Dotty's physicians and away from me. My function, as I saw it, was to support whatever choice Dotty made in conjunction with her physicians. I called the oncologist, and told him what had transpired. He said he'd talk things over with the surgeon and we'd discuss it during Dotty's visit the following week. In one sense, to use another cliche, I was relieved to have the great weight removed from my shoulders, but in larger measure, I was frightened that Dotty might have a recurrence of breast cancer.

On Tuesday at the oncologist's office, when Dotty was in the bathroom, her doctor passed me in the hall. "Did you speak to Ron (Dotty's breast surgeon)?" I asked.

He nodded. "We'll talk in the room."

After examining Dotty's breast, he flipped through the chart, then stood in front of her holding her hands. "I noticed that the lump increased in size on the sonogram, so I called Ron Sedgeway. He feels it should come out. Although unlikely, malignant cells could hide in the lump."

"What do you think?" Dotty asked.

"I have little experience with benign tumors. I don't usually see them unless they're malignant. I'll have to bow to Ron's judgement."

What a copout, I thought

"But the radiologist said fibroadenomas become cancer as often as pigs fly," Dotty said.

Her doctor shrugged.

"What choice do I have, none?" She turned to me while rubbing her eyes. "Don't you agree?"

I nodded as another cliche ran through my head—damned if you do, damned if you don't. "It seems to be the only safe choice."

After the doctor left the room, I stood up and put my arms around Dotty. "It will be okay. Let's put this behind us so we can get on with our lives."

She buried her head in my shoulder, then moved it up and down and sighed.

Dotty had another breast ultrasound that showed the size of her tumor had indeed increased—that the last ultrasound wasn't an anomaly. She had a consultation with her surgeon who outlined to her what he had said to me on the phone. We made arrangements for the surgery to be done in two weeks. First, Dotty would have to see her internist for surgical clearance, go to the hospital to preregister and have blood work, then see the anaesthesiologist to decide what type of anaesthesia she would receive, and to sign all the permission papers. Fortunately, they took us right away at each of these stops because I had taken care of the anaesthesiologist's and the receptionist's children. I was grateful because Dotty was too agitated to sustain a long vigil. Still, I felt sorry for the other people who had to wait for long periods of time.

After a string of questions, the anaesthesiologist smiled. "That's all," he said. "You can leave after signing these two permission forms."

Dotty picked up the first form. "What's this for?"

"Didn't Dr. Sedgeway tell you? On the day of surgery you have to go to the Women's Breast Center so that the radiologist can put a wire into the lump, under ultrasound, in order to localize it for the surgeon. It'll make the surgery more accurate, less disfiguring, and easier to do."

I saw Dotty's face become ashen. I had no knowledge this was to be done, but it sounded like a good idea to me. "It'll be okay. Go ahead and sign it," I said. "That's the way they do it now." I intended to check out the facts when we got home.

Then the anaesthesiologist handed her a form from the surgeon's office to sign permission to have the lump removed. "I'm not signing this," Dotty said.

I looked over her shoulder and saw that the permission was for a partial mastectomy. "I can't blame you," I said.

"I'll call Dr. Sedgeway's office," the anaesthesiologist said. When he finished talking, he turned to Dotty. "They said they'd change the permission to a lumpectomy and you can sign it on the day of surgery."

"What the Hell was that all about?" Dotty asked me as we were leaving.

"I guess, technically speaking, removal of any breast tissue is a partial mastectomy. But I bet phrasing it that way they can collect more from the insurance company. They don't seem to care that it might scare the Hell out of the patient."

"Well, I wasn't going to sign it."

I put my arm around Dotty who was shivering. "I know. You did the right thing."

Late in the afternoon on the day preceding surgery, I called, as we had been instructed, to find out what time we needed to be at the hospital for the wire placement and Dotty's surgery. The extension provided to me gave me immediate access to a human voice, unlike the day before Dotty's cancer surgery, when I waded through a potpourri of menus, waited for human contact for what seemed like an eternity, and then hung up in anger. That time, I called the surgeon at home to get the information we needed. The operating room clerk informed me that we had to be at the hospital by 5:30 A.M. to have the wire placed at 8:00.

"Why so early?" I asked.

"You know, paper work."

"And what time is the surgery?"

"Hard to say. Your wife is his second scheduled case. Usually about 10:00-10:30."

I thanked the clerk and told Dotty what I had learned. "I don't mind getting there early," she said. "As long as we get done quickly. They won't have to keep me a long time afterwards since I'm only getting twilight sleep. I'd like to be home between 12:00 and 1:00 for lunch."

"That would be nice, and of course with good news."

She smiled and we embraced.

That evening, we had dinner with my son, daughter-in-law, and four-year-old triplet grandchildren. When we came home there was a message on our answering machine to call the scheduling clerk in the operating room as there had been a change in plans. I dialed the extension and the phone rang and rang unanswered. What now, I thought? I dialed the main hospital extension and the operator tried to connect me to scheduling.

Dotty went to our bedroom to get ready for sleep. I realized the angst she must be feeling and hoped I'd be able to get off the phone quickly. I wanted to embrace her under the oil hanging over our bed that she had painted of us looking at *Moon River,* named for our song.

After the phone rang three or four times a melodious voice recording answered.

> *"Listen carefully. Our prompts have changed. If you are calling in regard to a billing question, press one now.*
> *"If you are calling in regard to our physician referral service, press two now."*

The curly cord twisted into knots. Dotty knew how to keep it straight—knew how to keep our world in order. Not at this juncture. I hoped the cliche deja vu bore no reality to our predicament, but I was angry, and frightened.

"If you are calling about laboratory or x-ray results, press three now.
"If you are calling to speak to a person and know the extension, dial it now. If not, press four now.
"If this is a physician, press five now."

I gripped the phone, angry at this nonsense keeping me from Dotty's side. "What's happening?" she called out.

"Just waiting to find out what there's been a change of plans means."

"If you are inquiring about a scheduling question, press six now."

My middle finger was poised above five, but I thought better about jabbing it. I might get another menu.

"To repeat the menu, press seven now.
"To speak to an operator, remain on the line or press zero."

This time I was wiser and didn't play the prompt game. I assaulted zero and asked the operator to connect me directly to the operating room. When the clerk answered, she told me to hold the line while she found out what the call was all about.

I bounced on the balls of my feet while I waited. Then held the phone over the cradle to hang up. The information might be important so I kept holding. The music playing was once again, Beethoven's *Ode to Joy.* I hoped this was a good omen and there was joy left for us.

In the bedroom, I heard Dotty weeping. The clerk got on the phone. "Sorry to keep you waiting so long."

I wanted to tell her she could shove the hospital up her ass, but this time held my tongue.

"Dr. Sedgeway has an emergency case he needs to put before your wife, but he still wants you here at 5:30 for the wire placement. Thought we'd let you know."

"Why does she have to be there so early then?"

"Because that's when the radiologist has the placement scheduled."

"You mean she has to lie around all day with a wire hanging out of her breast. You know this is an emotionally traumatic procedure."

"It's not so bad. There's no pain associated with the wire. We've done this a thousand times."

Not so bad for you I thought, not for you.

I smashed the phone into the cradle and went back to tell Dotty. For the first time I could remember, since her breast cancer, her once vibrant brown eyes were clouded and her impeccably coiffed bobbed hair was disheveled. I hugged her and we fell asleep entwined in each other's arms.

At 5:45 the next morning, we staggered into the admitting office having had only a few hours of sleep. After more paperwork, we were directed to the Women's Breast Center where I was told to stay in the waiting room while Dotty had her wire placed.

"Not going to happen," I said.

"Well, you can come in and wait in the anteroom of the changing area," the receptionist said. "But if it gets too crowded or when she goes into the exam room, you'll have to come back out here and wait."

I nodded. Like Hell, I thought.

The diminutive anteroom was full. I took my six-foot frame and buried it in a corner, as all the women stared at me. I remained like that until they came to take Dotty to the exam room.

"You'll have to wait out front," the technician said.

Before I could reply, the head of the unit walked into the hallway and we stared at each other. "Dr. Winick?" she asked.

I nodded. "How are you, Gloria? It's good to see you." I had cared for her two children.

After chatting for a few minutes, she turned to a colleague and introduced me, "Dr. Winick diagnosed a rare strep infection that saved my daughter's life."

If she says so, I thought. I had no recollection of that particular incident. However, I was not averse to taking advantage of her perception. "Do you think I could stay with my wife while they place this wire in her breast?"

She smiled. "Sure, no problem. We'll even stuff a chair into the corner for you."

I thanked her and joined Dotty in the exam room. When the radiologist came in, she looked at the ultrasound the technician was in the process of doing.

"Here to have that fibroadenoma removed?" the radiologist asked.

I pointed to the ceiling. "From your mouth to His ears."

"That's what it is," she said. "It has all the typical characteristics on the sonogram." She then used medical jargon to describe what she was seeing. If she was right, why was Dr. Sedgeway being so adamant? I hoped it wasn't to just cover his ass, afraid of a potential malpractice suit. That's the defensive kind of medicine I abhorred—the kind that drives up health costs and drives patients into a frenzy.

When the radiologist finished, I thanked her. A transportation aide wheeled Dotty to the preop area, where we waited and waited in a large room stuffed with people. There were few chairs available. I knew what cattle must feel like being herded into a pen. I stood, shifting my weight from foot to foot, standing behind a chair we managed to find for Dotty. As I walked toward the receptionist to find out what was taking so long, they called her name.

We were ushered into the preop area, where an intake nurse took a perfunctory history. Dotty was then strapped to a gurney and wheeled to a cubicle marginally wider than the gurney. This claustrophobic space was framed by two yellow curtains. She was hooked to all the monitors including one to her index finger to measure her blood's oxygen saturation. It made the finger glow like ET. A nurse came in and pierced Dotty's skin with a wide bore needle, threaded a catheter into her vein, and attached it to a bottle of fluid hanging from a pole. It was now 10:00.

"What now?" I asked.

"The anaesthesiologist will come talk to her before the surgery." She turned to Dotty. "If you need something to take the edge off, let me know."

"Let's just get this over with," Dotty said.

"How long?" I asked.

The nurse shrugged. "Hard to tell. Dr. Sedgeway is running way behind. A few hours at least."

I wondered why we had to be here so early. Was paper work and physician convenience more important than a patient's emotional well being? I listened to a young surgeon, who I cared for as a child, reaming out a nurse for not having his patient ready—for keeping him waiting. Didn't she know time was money? I hoped this wasn't the attitude of the majority of the modern generation of physicians.

To distract Dotty, we played Ghost and Superghost. Normally, her vocabulary which is vaster than mine, sealed a victory for her, but on that day her mind was focused elsewhere, allowing me to win. "Not bad for a guy who got brung up in Brooklyn," I said.

She smiled for the first time today. "Figured I had to let you win occasionally or you'd stop playing with me."

"Sure you did."

Despite the distraction, time crept like an infant learning to crawl. It was past 12:00 and Dotty was still not allowed to eat or drink. I refused to go down to the cafeteria and leave her.

Dr. Sedgeway breezed by. "Won't be much longer. This first case is a difficult one and is taking my partner and me longer than we expected." He turned to me. "Whipple procedure, but they're getting a second operating room ready for my use."

I knew the Whipple procedure was for pancreatic cancer and was a long, painstaking operation with little chance of success. I nodded.

When he left, Dotty was more agitated. "I wish we could just get this over with," she said.

"Don't worry. All this will seem like a bad dream, as long as the title of the Shakespearean play comes true." I smiled. *"All's Well That Ends Well."*

Dotty shifted position on the gurney. "My back is starting to hurt."

I put my hand in the small of her back and rubbed. "Better?"

She nodded.

At 2:00 the anaesthesiologist drifted in. "It won't be much longer now. The room's almost ready."

Dotty told her that she wanted as little twilight sleep as possible, and no anaesthesia.

"We'll do the best we can." She grasped Dotty's hand. "Don't worry. Everything will be fine."

How do you know, I thought? Do you know what the surgical pathology of Dotty's mass will show? "Thank you," I said.

Thirty minutes later, The nurse came to wheel Dotty into the operating room. I kissed her forehead and gave her the thumbs up sign. "See you in recovery," I said.

I watched till she was no longer visible, then headed for the surgical waiting room where I was told Dr. Sedgeway would come talk to me when he finished. On the way, I picked up two packages of nuts, then sat munching them while watching some inane soap opera. The droning of the TV caused my eyes to flutter shut. I dreamt about Sylvia. I was at her retirement party. She was a receptionist in my office for more than twenty years. Everyone was in a festive mood, but Sylvia was sullen.

"There's life after work," I said.

She nodded. "I know, but, but . . . ." Words didn't come, only tears to her eyes.

"What?"

She leaned forward and whispered. "I haven't told many people that I have breast cancer."

"I, I'm so sorry."

"Don't be. I'm going to lick it."

"Of course you will. You know if you need anything you can lean on me."

My dream flipped forward. I saw an ashen Sylvia with a pink hat covering her bald head. I saw a weak Sylvia, barely able to speak, comforting me when I told her of Dotty's breast cancer. I saw Dotty and me holding hands in the church a few months ago, while the priest eulogized Sylvia. Tears streamed from Dotty's eyes because of her sadness, and I wondered if she was contemplating her own mortality.

My eyes opened. I was shivering. I hoped Dotty's fate was different from Sylvia's. I looked at my watch. It had been an hour since they took Dotty to surgery. Where was Dr. Sedgeway? I asked the receptionist to see if my wife was out of surgery. She informed me that Dotty had just arrived in post-op. I could see her in about five minutes.

"Where's Dr. Sedgeway?" I asked aloud.

"I guess he'll see you there."

When I got to the recovery room, Dotty was really groggy. They must have given her more sedation than they planned or that she wanted. I kissed her on the forehead. "It's over," I said.

She tried to smile and speak, but only managed to stammer. "What did it show?"

"I don't know. I haven't seen Dr. Sedgeway. I'll ask the nurse if she can page him for me."

The nurse made a few calls and informed me that Dr. Sedgeway was doing another case. He would be in to see us when he finished.

"What did the biopsy show?" I asked.

"I don't know. He'll have to tell you."

After some prodding and, if truth be told, a little yelling, I convinced the nurse to put me through on the intercom to Dr. Sedgeway's operating room. His surgical assistant answered and I asked her to find out the results of Dotty's biopsy. I heard her relay the message to Dr. Sedgeway. His manner was surly. "I can't talk in the operating room. Tell him I'll be out to discuss it when I'm finished here."

I was convinced Dotty had a recurrence of her cancer. Otherwise, why wouldn't he just have said, everything is fine? I'll be out to see you when I'm done.

I returned to Dotty who was now more alert and her speech more intelligible. "What did you find out?" she asked.

"Nothing! He's doing another case and will be out to talk when he's finished."

"That's terrible."

"I know."

I held Dotty's hand and stared at the overhead clock, watching the second hand go around in circles just like our lives. Dotty and I were lost in our own thoughts. Time crept by as we waited for him to arrive.

When he came through the door, I squeezed Dotty's hand. I tried to read his face, but was clueless as to what he would say.

"I don't feel comfortable talking in the operating room." he said. "It isn't fair to the patient I'm working on."

Here it comes, I thought. It has to be bad news for him to say that.

"The biopsy showed only fibroadenoma, no sign of cancer."

I exhaled deeply and kissed Dotty on the forehead as she smiled. In my euphoria, I could hardly hear him giving her discharge instructions.

When he left, I took a few moments to reflect. I hoped now that we would be able to go on with our lives and enjoy retirement—that we would be able to sit in our condo and gaze at the magnificent view, while watching waves wash up on the shoreline. I knew, though, that the specter of breast cancer would always hover.

Chapter Twenty-One

–Shattered Dreams

We were getting our lives back to some semblance of normality, and were even traveling more. Dotty, and I were looking forward to this trip with a gusto we hadn't experienced for awhile. First we would fly to England, where we would visit family. I was glad that everyone there was well, and we would be able to see the family matriarch who was ninety-seven years old. I realized that this would probably be the last time we would see her alive, and was grateful for the opportunity.

After our visit to England, we were going to join good friends on a cruise from Dover to New York. Dotty and I would be celebrating our forty-fifth wedding anniversary and my seventy-first birthday. Unbeknownst to our friends, the trip would mark an even more significant anniversary for Dotty and me. We would be celebrating her ten year survival from breast cancer. At the time of her diagnosis, we had cancelled our dream trip to Australia, and I was hoping, in some small measure, this cruise would mark a new beginning—one free of the constant burden of living with that dreaded disease, and with the weight it had put on our shoulders.

On the morning of our trip, Dotty was apprehensive. She folded and refolded the same shirts three times. She didn't enjoy flying, viewing it only as a means to an end. We were flying to New York where we would stay overnight, before catching the morning flight to London. That way we wouldn't experience jet lag.

"Everything will be fine," I said. "After all, we're flying first class."

"Yeah, but . . ."

I put my arm around her. "Come on, be happy. Let's enjoy this trip."

She smiled. "Let's"

On the limo ride to the airport, I stared out the window, dazzled by the bright sunlight reflecting off the signs guiding us to the Miami Airport. I hoped this was a good omen for our trip, in contrast to what I viewed as the bad vibes being generated by hurricane Gustav and tropical storm Hannah churning in the Atlantic.

At the airport, my angst increased because we had to pay one hundred dollars for overweight luggage. "Big deal," Dotty said. "It's only money."

When we went through security, they confiscated my hair spray and Dotty's Listerine and deodorant. They were more than the maximum four ounces allowed. I could see Dotty was upset. "Big deal," I said. "It's only money."

We both smiled.

When we reached the gate, I suspected trouble. The waiting area was jammed with passengers stuffed into almost every available seat, surrounded by their carry-on luggage, but no representative from American Airlines was present. When the representative finally arrived, we were informed that the plane we were taking was late coming in from Peru, and there would be at least a two-hour delay in our flight. So, we settled down in our cramped seats, and while Dotty read, I listened to the sounds of the airport and the grumbling of our fellow passengers.

Across the way, sat a young man with dark toned skin and oriental features. I wondered if he could be of Filipino or Peruvian extraction. He was dressed in torn jeans and a frayed windbreaker. His long hair was askew over a somber face. He clung to a guitar like it was the last night of the world, loosening his grip only to remove a cell phone from his backpack and dial a number. He spoke in unaccented English. "Hey, Gino, it's me, Anthony. The damn plane has been delayed a couple of hours. I hope I get there in time for our gig, but it doesn't look like it. It was going to be our big break. You, Raymond, and Rahim might have to go on without me."

While listening, he shifted in his seat, and pulled the guitar closer. "I know the sound will be different. I know the trouble you had getting the agent to attend. But what can I do?"

I twisted my head so as not to seem obtrusive, but our eyes locked, and he shrugged. Then he laughed and shouted into the phone. "Wow, that Raymond is some crazy dude. He actually crashed that high brow gig and got tossed out on his ass. He's lucky they didn't call the police to throw him in jail"

After pausing to listen, Anthony continued. "What do you mean Raymond won't go on without me, and if he doesn't show, neither will Rahim? I'll try and get there, but . . . If Raymond doesn't show, I'll personally kick his ass. Tell him that."

Anthony turned his head away from me when he caught me staring. His loud voice dropped in volume, so I could barely hear what he said next. It sounded like, it isn't every day that you can open for the Sneeze Boxes, or something similar. Then his decibel level increased. "I'll get there if I can, but if I don't make it, you've got to get Raymond and Rahim to go on without me. I'm counting on you Gino."

After listening for a few more seconds, Anthony snapped the cell phone shut, clung to his guitar, and mumbled. "God damn this fuckin airline." He shook his head, as he and his guitar rocked back and forth in the seat.

My attention turned to an elderly couple, who were perhaps ten years older than Dotty and me. They grasped each other, as I strained to eavesdrop. Her disheveled, gray hair rested on his tufted, otherwise bald head. Dotty's eyes were fluttering shut, so I placed her head on my shoulder and stroked her temple.

The couple across the way looked glum. She looked up at him through tear stained eyes. "It's going to be close, but if we miss the connection to Barcelona, we'll have to stay overnight in New York. We'll miss the ship and our fiftieth anniversary cruise will be kaput."

"Don't be so pessimistic," he said.

"Pessimistic hell, I'm just plain angry. If the plane is any later than they say, I'm going to give the agent a piece of my mind. Maybe, they can call ahead and delay the Barcelona flight."

Her husband patted her head, which seemed temporarily to calm her. Fifteen minutes later though, when there were no further announcements, she stood and stormed to the desk. I saw her jawing with the agent, but couldn't hear what was being said.

When she came back, her husband looked up from the paper he was reading. "So?"

"So, nothing. It doesn't look like our plane will arrive in time to make our connection. They're calling ahead to try and hold our flight, but they won't guarantee anything."

I must have twitched, and Dotty's head jerked off my shoulder. "What's happening?" she asked.

I told her what I knew about the delay and whispered about the predicament of the couple across the way. "That's too bad," she said. "I'm glad we're not trying to make a connection tonight."

During the next hour, the woman wore the carpet thin by marching to the desk. Each time she returned with the same news—no definite decision had been made as to whether to hold the Barcelona flight if we arrived late.

A small, five or six-year-old, boy, sat down next to me. His skin was brown, and he wore a red tee-shirt. His sad look tore at my heart. As always, I viewed it as my mission to cheer a child up. How could I as a pediatrician fail to do that? I extended my palm, face up. "Slap me five," I said.

He reached over, trying to smash his palm into mine, but I withdrew and scratched my nose. "I have an itch."

I extended my palm again. "Try again." I withdrew my palm again, as he hit nothing but air, and I scratched his nose. "Looks like you have an itch this time."

He laughed.

After several more misses, I looked into his eyes. "Are you teasing me?"

He spoke with a squeaky voice, in a Carribean accent. "No, you're doing it."

On his next try our palms made contact. "Gotcha," he said.

"You're too good for me. By the way, where's your wife?" I asked.

"I'm too little." Then he circled his index finger around his temple. "You're cuckoo."

"Then who are you with?"

"My auntie and grandma." He pointed to a brightly clad, middle-aged woman, sitting on the floor, her back against a wall. Then he turned around and pushed his index finger in the direction of a stout, gray-haired woman arrayed all in black. She smiled at him, and he waved.

"We're going to visit my mama. She's in the hospital, but she's getting better."

"That's good," I said.

"Auntie promised me, we could visit her tonight."

I nodded. With the plane being so late, we wouldn't arrive until at least eight. By the time the luggage came and they drove to the hospital, it would be beyond the visiting time of most hospitals. I could see how eager the boy was to see his mother, and how disappointed he would be if that didn't happen tonight. I had many questions I wanted to ask—what's wrong with your mother? How long has she been in the hospital? But since it was none of my business and I didn't want to put the little guy through the third degree, I remained silent. He already had enough of a burden to bear.

His aunt stood up and walked over to us. Her loose fitting, yellow dress, hid a full figure. "I hope he's not bothering you," she said.

"On the contrary, we're having fun."

"I was watching you. Thank you for distracting him."

"I know. He told me his mother is in the hospital."

Her smile faded, and she leaned over and whispered. "My sister's quite ill, cancer. We're hoping for the best."

"Good luck," I said.

She turned to the little boy. "Come Ziggy, don't bother the nice man anymore."

I bent down so I made eye contact with Ziggy. "You weren't any trouble. In fact, thank you for playing with me."

He smiled, grasped his aunt's hand, and they walked back to his grandmother.

As I sat down next to Dotty, the American Airlines representative made an announcement. "The plane from Peru just landed. It will take about thirty minutes to refuel, clean, and restock the plane. We have a full flight, so if you quickly follow the boarding procedure, we can be on our way as soon as possible. For those of you who have connections to make in New York, we are trying to find out what's happening. So far, we have been unable to confirm anything. We will keep trying and let you know what we find out once we're in the air."

I turned to Dotty. "I hope this delay doesn't put a damper on some of these people's dreams—that it will turn out to be an annoyance rather than a dream breaker."

"Me too. I know first hand how fate can shatter your dreams."

I nodded, and put my arm around Dotty, as we sat back to await the boarding process.

When we were called, there was a mad dash to the gate. Passengers jockeyed and jostled for position, anxious to be on their way. The pushing and shoving slowed the boarding, causing us to leave even later. Sitting across the aisle from us was the elderly couple trying to make a Barcelona connection so they wouldn't miss their fiftieth anniversary cruise. The woman kept looking at her watch and shaking her head.

"What time is your next flight?" I asked

"Seven-forty-five," she said.

"Will they hold the flight?"

She shrugged. "I hope so."

If we were on schedule, we would land at eight, fifteen minutes after the Barcelona plane was scheduled to take off. No wonder the woman kept shaking her head and incessantly grumbled into her husband's ear.

Dotty and I toasted each other with our glasses of champagne. "To a wonderful trip," I said. "To your tenth anniversary of surviving breast cancer. To us."

"I'll drink to them all." We clinked glasses.

I closed my eyes and hoped that unlike the people we had encountered, nothing would dampen this trip for us—a trip meant as a new beginning, and meant to put the zest back in our lives.

The trip to New York was smooth and touched down on time, seven-fifty-nine. No information was given to passengers who were making connections. They were told to meet at the American Airlines counter where we deplaned. As we taxied toward the gate, the woman across the aisle tapped my shoulder. "We're pulling into gate forty," she said. "The Barcelona flight is leaving from gate thirty-eight. Could you please look out the window and see if there's a plane there when we pass?"

I nodded and stared through the pane. There was a plane at gates thirty-four and thirty-six, but as we approached gate thirty-eight, I could see it was empty.

When I told the woman, she raised her voice. "Damn, we've missed our connection. Damn American Airlines. Damn, Damn, Damn." She turned to her husband and buried her face in his shoulder.

An announcement was made to let the passengers taking connecting flights deplane first. A lot of good it will do for the couple next to us, I thought.

As we walked to retrieve our luggage, Ziggy ran up to me, slapped my hand and whizzed by. His aunt hurried to catch him. As she passed me, she slowed. "Thanks again for entertaining my nephew."

"Will you be able to get to the hospital tonight?"

She shook her head, and ran after Ziggy.

Before we reached the end of the concourse, Anthony, who had been in the back of the plane, passed us. A cell phone was glued to his ear, a backpack was slung over his shoulder, and he clung to the guitar with his free hand.

As he raced by, I overheard him scream into the phone. "Because of a fuckin flight delay, we've blown our chance." He soon was too far ahead for me to hear anything else.

As I stood by the carousel waiting for our luggage, I prayed that the hope and dream I envisioned for our trip, and the rest of our lives, wouldn't be shattered like the hopes and dreams of the people we had encountered in the Miami Airport.